Constant Pursuit

Correcting the Word Coincidence for What It Really Is: An Act of God

Erica Hedtke Barreto

ISBN: 978-1-0983-6638-4

www.ericahedtkebarreto.com
IG: @ericahedtkebarreto
Twitter: @ericahedtkebarreto

Chapter Index

To Beth, who has been a beautiful example of God's love.

Prologue

When you chose this book, what were you looking for? Hope? Inspiration? Something for your commute? I hope you'll find each of those things here.

Wherever you are in your own life and faith journey, know that it wasn't a coincidence that you are reading this right now. I'm going to challenge you to look at the word *coincidence* for what it really is, God's hands at work.

If you think it's a coincidence that you got this book from a friend; it wasn't. If you think it was a coincidence that it was directly in front of you at the bookstore; it wasn't. The stories you are going to read are factual, heart-warming stories of faith that only God could have orchestrated.

This book may not be like any other story you've read, and just know, that was on purpose. After reading hundreds of Christian books in the marketplace, I craved a book filled with testimonies of how God works in the daily. And thus, *Constant Pursuit* was born.

You'll see my inner dialogue sprinkled within chapters, helping readers see when I began noticing these "coincidences." You'll also notice that not every chapter is the same length, because in a non-fiction tale, God doesn't design our stories to have three-hundred-word consistency, even though modern publishing would love it to be that way.

I pray that this book will inspire you to investigate your own life and see where God has been silently working in the background. I pray that this book will make you smile because you feel encouraged, knowing that you too can have these experiences with our Creator. If you've been going through life feeling like you must be someone special for God to show up, I'm here to tell you that you are beyond extraordinary, and the wait is over.

I ask that you take this walk with me over the duration of this book to reflect on your own life to see where God has been calling you to find your purpose. Or maybe this book will be there, putting a smile on your face, as you read the story of a dreamer. Whatever it may do for you, thank you for being here.

Whether this book is your cup of tea or not, I pray that you will pass it along so that others can begin unraveling the mystery of who their maestro is. I pray you become an advocate for Christ, shouting from the rooftop how you became inspired on your own journey, as testimonies are an extremely powerful tool at our disposal. I pray that you'll go write an incredible review for your sister in Christ, as your way of showing your love and support.

This book is un-coincidentally and uniquely the book that you were meant to see in this moment, and nothing else. I hope you enjoy.

Where It All Began

I had just gotten home from another three-hour dance practice when I went into my room, slammed the door, threw my body onto my twin-sized bed, and reached for the remote. Before I could find *That's So Raven*, I stumbled upon a scene of four gorgeous women all sipping drinks at some cool, dimly lit, crowded spot with their beautiful clothes and fancy purses. I couldn't peel my eyes away. There was something about the way they were bonding, about the confidence they each had, and the way others seemed to be attracted to them. As I was watching, there was one girl in particular that I became enamored with.

Not only did we have similar appearances, but she too was a fashionista, just like I aspired to be. It was as if I were meeting my grown-up, sophisticated doppelganger but with way more accessories. Watching her have it all proved to me that not only was it possible, but if I worked hard enough, I could have that too. I could have a fabulous career, best girlfriends, sophistication, all living in the big city, just like her.

Her name was Carrie Bradshaw. After watching every episode over and over until I could recite the words, I declared to my family and friends that my dream was to move to New York City and be like Carrie.

I was now twelve years old.

As for me, I was awkward. I had just joined a new school with a bunch of kids that seemed to only wear Hollister, crop tops, and judgement. Meanwhile, I had peaked far earlier than most and subsequently was the tallest, lankiest girl in my class, sprouting boobs far too early and still repping the once juvenile Aeropostle. Physically, I felt like an eyesore, but internally, I always felt like a passionate girl, wanting to shout my dreams from the rooftop.

Trying to get immersed into a new school and this white suburbia, my mom signed me up for dance six days out of the week as a way of getting familiar with new kids and the town. While I liked dance, I only cared about one thing...fashion. I wanted to be like my icon, Carrie; fashionable, desired, and successful.

At this age, my parents had already been divorced and remarried for over ten years. Much of my time I spent with my mom, stepdad Gary (cue Jimmy Fallon), and my two sisters. Like most red blooded, middle class families, we did the typical things. We went camping a few times a month, took annual school shopping trips, and ate dinner together. When we girls weren't fighting over clothes or AOL time, we loved each other very much.

But the one thing we didn't do was attend church. It wasn't that we didn't believe in God; it's just that we didn't talk about Him. We were those unspoken Christians, I suppose. It was like we knew we were good people and that we believed in God, but He never entered our home or conversations. And for me, that was the norm.

Every other weekend, however, I would spend time with my dad. My dad always proved two constants in my life: I was his number one gal and having a relationship with God meant everything. My dad was always 'Mr. Cool,' sporting leather pants, fast sports cars, and rocking out as the lead guitarist at our church. I would spend hours those weekends with him at church, just watching the band practice before anyone else arrived. I stared admiringly and sat patiently listening to those modern songs until I saw the band packing up, which was my cue to jump on stage to offer my assistance. My dad would always share with me who God was and what His unconditional love looked like.

"Erica, God will always love you because He thinks you are perfect, and so do I! You can never lose God's love; It's unconditional and so is mine!" he would gleam with joy.

Based on what my dad said, I believed God loved me no matter what I did or no matter what I did wrong, but I really didn't know anything else about Him. Though I had officially given my life to Christ while I attended the Christian concert *Acquire the Fire* with my close friend, Ashley, I didn't know what was next.

With all my time spent at church with my dad, I was never baptized or enrolled in any classes, so when I was sitting, admiring my dad on stage, passively listening to the message, everything felt very over-my-head. When I was inactively sitting at church hearing about Jonah and the whale or Jesus parting the Red Sea, it all felt like folklore or Greek mythology. And while I was curious about those stories and the Bible, I also thought that the hand I was dealt didn't allow me the resources to figure it out. I was fine knowing that it was what it was, and at least, God would love me regardless, because He made me.

* *

Entering high school, it was hard enough to blend in with the gossipy lunch tables, clichés, and the unspoken rules of coolness. I knew without a doubt, it definitely wasn't cool to talk about curiosities about God or sharing big dreams like wanting to be the next Carrie Bradshaw. So, I didn't. I kept my dreams and desires to myself, only sharing those private inner thoughts with my family and close friends, almost like I was ashamed of it. But in my heart of hearts, I knew that one day I would make it to New York, as well as dip my toe into learning more about this mysterious man in the clouds.

Now entering into my high school years, I was still all eyes on the prize with my dream of being in fashion and moving to NYC. But the reality was, I had never worked in fashion and didn't know where to start. I was under the assumption Target and Hérmes were doing the same thing.

****

I had just fallen out of yet another waitressing job and was desperately needing to find new work. As I was scrolling through Google's options, I came across a genre of business that I hadn't thought about before; bridal. I found a cute bridal salon about twenty minutes from home and thought it might be a good fit. Thinking to myself how cool it would sound to work there, I jumped in my mom's '06 Murano and immediately headed to the store to see if they were hiring.

I walked in and saw nothing but white: white walls, white gowns, and white shoes. I saw an older, plump woman with a glowing smile near the register, so I headed her way with what I can only imagine was a pretty sad resume. With a giant smile on my face, I spoke with her for several minutes, explaining that I had no experience in selling bridal dresses but I felt this was the position for me, along with the fact that I needed hours and was eager to learn. Gloria, with her wide gap in between her teeth, explained to me that just mere moments before my arrival she was praying to the Lord to send someone to their shop because they were in desperate need of an employee. She had even asked for this new employee to be a woman of faith and to brighten up their store.

*Interesting, I thought. It did seem rather coincidental how I found her shop so easily and how right away she mentioned God in our conversation, at a point in my life when I still didn't know much about who He was. *

Gloria added, "You know, you have a smile that would surely brighten up anyone's day!" Within a matter of ten minutes, she hired me for the position. Shaking my head over how easy the whole transaction was, I sailed away, knowing I'd be back a few days later to soak in all I could about working in a bridal salon.

It was a Tuesday morning and I was eager to jump in. On my first day, I was shown by a sweet and soft-spoken high schooler how to assist in picking wedding dresses for brides and how to steam the dresses before they went out on the floor.

As I left for the day, I rang my mom and told her, "I think I just opened Narnia's closet!"

While I was feeling like I was getting the hang of this new job, my boss felt otherwise. I got called in to talk in private with Gloria and was told, "We love having you here, but I just don't think you're picking it up as quickly as I would have liked."

I was headed for the door with only six months' work experience under my belt. This was the first job I had gotten let go from, but I knew that I was too interested in bridal to let it slip away that easily.

*Some feeling in my heart told me that this wasn't the end of that saga. Hmmm.... *

Needing to get another job quickly, I started working at the local watering hole, taking customer orders, bussing tables, and juggling way too many sections. I excelled as a waitress and enjoyed doing it because of all the faces, personalities, and multi-tasking that the job required. But, while I was running like a mad woman on a busy afternoon shift with only two servers, I couldn't help but feel like I really needed to make my way back into fashion, especially if I ever wanted to consider making it in New York one day.

I knew then that I really needed to get my resume built up; otherwise, New York would laugh in my face. But I just didn't know how or where to begin.

* *

In my third period, I passively listened to Olivia, my Spanish teacher, talk about verb endings. She abruptly changed the topic, as she too must have noticed all the blank stares out the window and doodling happening in notebooks. She announced that she would be taking fifteen students to Costa Rica over the summer as an immersion experience that would count for credit. She explained that there would be an informational meeting after school on Friday in room D140 for anyone interested. For some strange reason, I felt this huge desire to go and see what it was all about.

*Hmmm, that's interesting as I was not at all interested in Spanish and my grade definitely reflected that... *

I went home and joyfully skipped around my mom, telling her random Costa Rica facts and the benefits of going. With an inquisitive look on her face yet a touch of being worn down, she begrudgingly agreed to go to the meeting with me. On Friday, we sat in the meeting, listening to past students share their testimonies, as well as the cost of the trip.

"Costa Rica was amazing! The monkeys, the fruit, and the home stay was like, totally rad!" exclaimed the guy who was clearly in the smoker's group at school. I was 100% all in, but let's just say it wasn't my wallet that would be footing the bill.

When we got out of the meeting, I jumped for joy like a toddler, exclaiming, "Mom, please can I go? Please! I really, really want to go. I'll fundraise. I'll sell stuff. Please!"

A few days later, probably because I wore her down, she agreed. With us both knowing that Spanish wasn't my best subject, and that's putting it lightly, I signed up under the agreement that I would try my absolute best and come out a stronger speaker than before. Having had three years of Spanish under my belt, I figured this trip would be a breeze and give me a nice tan, if nothing else.

Just a few weeks later, I was all signed up and ready to be shipped off on my first international adventure. We headed to San Juan where we would spend two and a half weeks jumping around different hotels and doing different excursions while the last two and a half weeks would be spent in a family stay.

I made good friends from that trip, hiked up inactive volcanoes, played outdoor games in the courtyards of our hotel, and tried out all the local hot springs. I equally enjoyed living with a completely normal Latin family with a similar dynamic to mine.

I absolutely loved Costa Rica; the gorgeous brown skinned people, beans and rice, the lush trees, and the monkeys that seemed to be everywhere. From that trip on, I knew that I needed to continue seeing other parts of the world, especially outside my Midwest bubble.

*Where did this intense desire come from all the sudden? I never dreamed of this before... *

While I was confident that I wanted to see more international environments, another thing I knew with my whole being was that I never wanted to speak Spanish. Ever again. Had it not been for my classmates in high school and those students in Costa Rica, I never would have passed.

Falling Apart

When I got home from Costa Rica, I entered into my senior year of high school. A lot of excitement was in the air. This was my year of getting my own car, entering a new sort of freedom, and being one step closer to my dream of moving to New York City. I returned home, borrowed the Gun Metallic Murano, and rushed to my dad's house to tell him all about how my trip went. The day ahead of us was an exciting one because we were going car shopping and for the first time, it was for me.

After hours and hours filled with greasy salesmen, rows of colored cars, and double decker's from Taco Bell, exhausted, I headed back home. I went straight to my mom's room to brag about how awesome it was looking at cars and daydreaming about owning a cherry-colored Toyota Corolla when I got interrupted by the phone ringing. I ran into my sister's hot pink bedroom to get the phone when I noticed it was my dad on the other line. I figured that I must have left something at his house, so I clicked on the phone before realizing that my mom picked it up moments before me. I stayed quiet for a moment so I wouldn't interrupt, but then the conversation took a weird turn.

"Hi Greg. How was today?"

Cutting her off, he let out, "I can't deal with Erica. She's a f*$%ing brat. You guys can figure it out and buy her the car!" he said with total exhaustion and frustration in his voice as he continued on.

I quickly hung up the phone, threw it on the floor, and went running to my room with a mixture of tears and snot running down my face. How could he say that about me? I've never heard him speak badly about me, much less say something so nasty.

Haven't I been everything he's ever wanted, sitting quietly while he's up on stage with his guitar at church, waiting around dealerships while he buys his latest toys, being dragged from car lot to car lot to gush about the latest models? And now, I'm the brat? Where had I been a brat in all of this? Were just a few hours of being with me that terrible for him, especially when the attention wasn't on him?

My mom saw this all play out like a predictable rom-com as she heard the other line beep. She came in to rub my back and offer tissues as she had so many times in the past. She had seen it time and time again; like, when he said he would be there and wasn't or when he would say that thoughtless comment about the way I looked with my hair pulled back. But this one ran deep, like the refried bean layer in his precious double deckers, deep.

****

Trying to push my feelings aside, I continued into my senior year. At school that week they were pulling the seniors into the counselors' office to confess what it was we wanted to do after graduation.

I sat down with Mr. Datrick, and like a naive kid with a huge bout of confidence, answered his question, "I'm going to study fashion and move to New York!"

He gave me the same condescending chuckle that everyone else did and said, "Okay... and what exactly does that mean? What type of job in fashion? What are you planning on studying in college and where are you applying?"

Feeling like I may have bitten off more than I could chew with those questions, I told him I didn't know but that I would surely narrow it down soon with an "I'll show you" smirk. I knew I had this burning desire to make these dreams come true, even if no one else believed or had faith.

*So deeply to my core did I know this was what I wanted to do with my life. Wonder where that came from... *

It was my weekend to spend with my dad and I was already pacing the living room, waiting to see his C-class Mercedes show up in the driveway. He didn't know I heard him on the phone the week before and I didn't want to bring it up, so I proceeded to act like the good daughter I thought I always was.

Our time together was comparable to all the other times; we went cruising around town in his latest souped-up ride, stopping at occasional car dealerships for both him and me, though in my heart, I knew it wasn't the same. His upbeat and supportive attitude remained as if everything was normal, but my hurt was fresh like a recent fall off a bicycle.

Throughout the day he reminded me that he loved spending time with me and that I was the love of his life, so slowly, I was coming around. I even opened up to him about my Costa Rica trip and about my snooty counselor who must have been out to get me with all of those ridiculous questions.

In the past when I shared with him that I wanted to move to NYC, he was very supportive and was the only one who didn't make me think I was living in fairytale land.

After that hang out, I was feeling almost back to our normal dynamic and in my mind, excused his behavior because I don't know, maybe I was being a teenage monster or maybe I misheard him when he promised the car. Either way, I wanted to put all the red flags and hurt behind me and move forward like I had done so many times in the past. But that wasn't quite what happened the next time I saw him.

****

Multiple failed marriages later, my dad had recently married a woman named Beth, who he had met only months prior, online. Beth seemed nice enough, though as a teenager, I had no interest in another "mommy" type coming into my life.

Just two months into marital bliss, my dad called me on a Thursday evening to share some news.

"Next month, we are going to be moving out of state so we can be closer to Beth's family."

He shared the news so fast, like he was ripping off a band aid and hoping for no hair to be attached.

Feeling incredibly confused, isolated, and full of questions that he was going to leave me for another woman, I said through my tears and blotchy redness, "But what about me? You can't leave me, I'm your only daughter! Doesn't that mean anything?"

Like a soulless creature who had practiced this conversation over and over, his response shattered my soul.

"She's my wife. I will always love her more than you."

It felt like I had dropped off a 1000-foot cliff and was mere moments from the pavement. I had set my dad on such a pedestal of this man who could do no wrong, who was so loving, so supportive, and a Godly man. Within a matter of moments, that all changed. I was disposable, like last week's salmon in the trash.

After that conversation, I looked backwards wondering what it all meant and questioning every conversation and all the feelings I've ever had. What had I done to deserve this type of punishment? Did he really mean it all those times when he said I love you? Did he really mean it when he said I was his number one gal? Was he really stuck in traffic all those times that he said he couldn't make it to my recitals?

Everything I knew about God; I knew because of my dad. Was God practicing a conditional love with me, just like him? Would God get sick of me and flick me off like a booger, just like him? Who was God then?

I was in the eye of the tornado, questioning everything about myself and how I loved and trusted.

I questioned, "Why me?" and "What could I have done differently to be more loved by him?" I questioned if everything about why my dad had lashed out on me was my fault. I questioned what was real and what was just an act. I questioned if God even loved me, because clearly, I was an unlovable beast, worthy of second place. I lost my identity.

If I wasn't Kim Kardashian-style crying to my mom, I was lashing out at the ones closest to me for any input they may have had. I was in a dark place where I didn't understand what was up from down or who did and didn't love me, for me. Feeling like I had lost all control, I did the one thing I thought could help me.

I borrowed mom's SUV and headed to church, hoping there would be a magic bean fix waiting for me when I got there.

Interesting that that's where I first thought to go...

I returned to the church that my dad played at, hoping to learn more about an ever-lasting Father who wouldn't leave or forsake me, like my earthly one. I wanted to learn outside of what my dad said, outside of bits and pieces I had heard. I wanted to find out for myself who God was and what a relationship with Him could look like.

I craved it like those people in Snickers commercials crave chocolate caramel. I felt so low at that point that I figured I had nothing left to lose by pouring my heart out to God through prayer and waiting for His response. Mind you, the waiting part was torture.

While I was continuing my own spiritual journey, my mom recommended that I go speak to a therapist about all the emotions I was feeling about my earthly father. I reluctantly went to meet with Dr. Molly for our introduction session where I told myself I would start slowly, like a first date. As this was my first time going to therapy, I wasn't quite sure what to expect, and judging by her office filled with fake ferns and colorfully distracting objects, I figured it would be a waste of time.

Dr. Molly started by asking innocently, "What do you want to talk about today?" and "What is causing you pain?"

Within moments, my eyes were swollen, my lips puffy, and I was sniffling through every word.

Through these sessions, we worked through the hurt and pain, and she helped me see that it was never about me. It was never something that I did. It was never something I could have done differently. It was just about a guy who is dealing with his own problems, and unfortunately, I came into the crosshairs. As for my new-stepmom Beth, I blamed her for everything and never even attempted to get to know her or her side of the story.

I also learned not to put all my admiration into one person like that, as that isn't their role. She went on to say that every time, that person is going to fail us.

Alongside counseling, I attended church and learned that God will never let me down, that He is my Father and that I should only be putting Him on a pedestal because He is the only Almighty being.

Between therapy, attending classes like *Alpha,* and finding out who God was, everything was beginning to make sense. I started to understand that I crowned my dad in a position that was never meant to be his and therefore, he was bound to let me down. I was beginning to see what the hype was with God and not through what my parents had told me or through bits and pieces of random information but through His word.

Eight months later after meeting with Dr. Molly and going through crash courses of spirituality, I came out a new person with hardly anything remaining in my tear ducts. Emotionally, it was my Everest, making it the hardest thing I've ever gone through.

However, it was also the time when I sought, questioned, and found God. As cliché as it sounds, I had to hit rock bottom to get me to this new beautiful place of forgiveness, self-healing, and a newfound relationship with Christ. *James 1:12 illustrates it best, *"Blessed is the one who perseveres under trial because, having stood the test, that person will receive the crown of life that the Lord has promised to those who love him."*

After being estranged from both my dad and Beth for over six months, I wrote a letter to both of them as the final exercise from Dr. Molly describing how I felt, why I took space apart, and that I was no longer holding onto that hurt or anger. I explained that the moment God came into my life, He took that off my shoulders as that is His burden to carry, not mine. I said, slowly, I would work to rebuild our relationship, just like I was building a new relationship with my Eternal Father in Heaven. I also apologized to Beth for never giving our relationship a chance.

*I was beginning to piece it together. Even though I went through something very tough, God used it to bring me closer to Him, which was the plan all along. I think I'm really beginning to love this God fellow. *

Putting all of that behind me, I was more than ready for the next chapter in my life: College!

*NLT version

Forever Changed

I had applied to five colleges after high school and amazingly got accepted to all of them. My first choice was the Arts Institute in Chicago. I still wasn't sure of what specifically in fashion I wanted to study, but I had faith I'd figure it eventually.

Faith, I'd figure it out…hmmm, maybe I am starting to get this God thing after all… *

I entered into a community college one month after graduating high school and just focused on taking my generals. I took random classes like politics, theology, and art literature, and became so frustrated because I knew none of these classes would help me in my future.

I would think to myself, "How is Intro to Microsoft going to help me when I'm working in fashion?"

During my time at this school, I had a bad attitude. Though I excelled at my classes, made a lot of friends, was involved in clubs and learned about topics I wouldn't have ever had a chance to learn about, I couldn't help but feel sorry for myself at the opportunities I missed.

About a year into school, it seemed painfully obvious that I was going to have to be more specific about how I defined "being in fashion." Over and over the school system would ask, "What does that mean? What specifically do you want to do? What kind of job will that get you? What will you specifically study?"

So, I started reading about job descriptions online, researched salaries, I talked with advisors at school to find out what job would best fit my skills and passions, and took my mom's advice to dive into the field by getting a job. At this point I had just moved closer to school so again, I needed to find a job.

I had prayed to God asking, "Lord, what is it I'm going to study? What job am I going to get? Help show me because right now, I have no clue."

One day as I was surveying the area I had just moved into; I came across a wedding store. Something *wink, wink* told me to go inside and ask if they were hiring. I then had this thought that, "why wouldn't they hire you; you have experience?"

With all this sudden confidence, I strolled in, found an older woman at the counter, and explained myself. I told her that I was new to the area, was needing work, and had some experience selling wedding dresses. This beautiful older fox of a woman shared with me that she had been praying for someone to come into the store seeking a job and she wanted someone with a fresh perspective. Within minutes, she had hired me.

*That's funny, I thought. That is exactly what the first bridal store owner said. *

Days later, I began working at the salon and felt like I was truly finding my place. I learned all about the different designers, good sales techniques to sell the gowns, back-end costs of the dresses, and other tricks of the trade. I quickly caught on and really wanted to make a difference in their store. I wanted to increase their sales and improve their customer experience process.

Every day working with brides felt like a hidden scavenger hunt and I was the one who helped find the prize! Each day was new and exciting, never looking the same as the day before. There was one day, especially, that I will never forget.

It was around 3:30 one bright Sunday afternoon when I was working alone at the bridal salon. It was a rather slow day until...they walked in! Two beautiful twins came into the store, both engaged, both shopping for dresses but both not enthused. Right away, I couldn't peel my eyes away from Tanya.

Tanya was dainty, quiet, and seemingly fearful of the experience. Her twin, Sandra, couldn't be more opposite. She was energetic, thrilled, and ready to try on dresses. As I politely asked both their wedding dates, ideas, and what types of dresses they had in mind, Tanya barely gave me any information. As Sandra was trying to be the cheerleader and encourage her twin to try on wedding dresses, she kept getting push back. As the consultant, I simply listened, smiled, and encouraged. I proceeded with Sandra, asking her to point out the dresses she liked and went through the motions but ultimately, I was enamored by Tanya.

Once Sandra was done trying on dresses and had found her top favorites, we both naturally turned it over to Tanya. Slowly, Tanya let out small pieces of information that would make up the puzzle that was her. Piece by piece and jag by jag, I found out that Tanya was recovering from a double mastectomy and had recently overcome thyroid cancer, all while having a rare life-threatening celiac disease that only made each of these earlier conditions more problematic. Oh, and did I mention she had a newborn, whilst dealing with all these medical conditions?

I was gentle and patient with her for several minutes until tears finally came strolling down her face as she let out her vulnerability.

"I don't want to get too excited or plan anything because I don't think I'm going to make it to my wedding day."

*Boom! That was quite a communication bomb. *

Feeling like I was out of breath, I watched as she ran her fingertips gently along the wedding dresses, almost like a little girl whose mom just told her she couldn't have a single toy at the local Toys' R' Us.

The store I worked for carried about twenty-five dresses, and there was one dress that she went back to over and over. The dress was a Mikaela by Paloma Blanca, ivory A-line gown with thin lace straps, lace bodice, and a sheen satin skirt with a beautiful champagne colored sash at the natural waist. It was one of my personal favorites because it was so timeless. While touching the gown, she stopped, and let out, "This is beautiful," as she proceeded to frown, almost trying to convince herself not to love it.

After what felt like ages of doing the same routine down the aisle of dresses, only to keep getting stopped at that particular Mikaela gown, I asked Tanya to just humor us by trying on that one dress she kept going back to. After much persistence from Sandra, Tanya obliged.

I could feel the tension in the air like watching someone who got caught cheating on their math assignment, while waiting for her to come out of the dressing room.

Moments later, she came out of the dressing room in a rather floating type of manner. I helped her step up on the pedestal in front of the three-way mirror and simply admired her, alongside her twin.

Words could not express how beautiful Tanya looked in that moment, in that dress. When she first saw a glimpse of herself, she couldn't help but twirl and imagine 'what if'.

For quick moments, we all fell in love with her in that dress. We fell in love with her smile, that rare but contagious smile that showed off her perfectly straight teeth. We fell in love with hope; hope that she could one day wear that dress as she walked down the aisle to the man she loved.

As the bridal consultant, trying to keep it on course, I said what I felt, "You look so beautiful. You're glowing!" while seamlessly grabbing a veil so she could envision what it all could look like on her wedding day. Her twin chimed in with, "Oh Tanya, you are beautiful!"

As tears strolled down Sandra's cheeks, something changed in Tanya. It was as if the enemy was whispering in her ear at the exact moment we were speaking out loud. Tanya quickly resorted back to her original stance of saying that she needed to take it off because she wasn't going to be able to wear such a beautiful gown for the occasion. She hurried back to the dressing room, taking off the dress and changed back into her light blue jeans and loose-fitting sweater. When she came back out of the dressing room, Sandra was urging her to remember how she felt and looked in that dress.

Tanya stayed firm, however, with her one-track mind and feeling so confident that her RIP date would approach much quicker than her wedding date.

The two girls stayed chatting with me long after they had tried on dresses, and an additional two hours after we had closed. I don't know why they felt the need to keep speaking to the stranger at the bridal store, but I felt in on my heart to be patient and to listen.

*Where did that feeling come from, I wondered? *

And, I did just that. I listened intently to every word as if there was going to be a quiz about it later. Tanya talked about her life with her new baby girl and fiancée, what she used to do for work before she got too sick to be able to continue the tasks, where she lived, and other details of her life. Sandra chimed in too with details of her life, but nothing took the focus like Tanya and her story.

As we were all making small talk, the two girls mentioned that in the next month, they were going to be hosting a benefit for Tanya, in hopes of raising enough money to help with her medical expenses. They went on to say it was going to be about an hour away in a small town they grew up in, but they would love if I came.

I don't know what made them invite me. Maybe they were just being nice, thinking that the more people they invite, the more money they would raise. Maybe it was a blanket invitation, thinking I wasn't going to go. Or maybe they invited me because our conversation naturally led us there. Either way, I felt in on my heart to go and I told them that.

Later that night, I had the hardest time sleeping. I tossed and turned as I prayed to God asking, "Lord, why did we cross paths?" and, "What am I supposed to do with this information?"

After what seemed like hours, I finally fell asleep and had visions dance in my head. I woke up with what can only be described as a lightbulb flashing over me like a neon sign. I had complete clarity about what I was to do next and what I was meant to do for Tanya. I knew exactly what God wanted. It's that gut type of feeling.

I called my mom, full of excitement, to tell her the whole story about what had happened the night before and what I was going to do moving forward. I told her that yesterday at work, I met a set of twin girls who were both engaged and that one of them had a full suitcase of illnesses she was facing. Because of it, she didn't think she was going to be alive for her wedding day.

I proceeded, "Mom, I know what I'm supposed to do for Tanya. I'm going to buy her that wedding dress that she loved and bring it to her benefit."

On the other end of the phone was silence. Sure, it was a lot of information to take in, but it wasn't quite the excitement I was hoping for. From there, the questions came pouring out.

"You're going to do what for a complete stranger? How are you going to afford this $3500 dress as a college student, and in only one month? Why do you feel you have to do this? And what if she really doesn't make it?" My mom had a way of putting a halt to my crazy ideas with rationality and reason. I didn't quite see it that way.

Valid questions, sure. From an outside perspective, I was a broke college student and had just met Tanya the night before, but without a doubt, God placed this desire on my heart and no matter how crazy it seemed, I knew with God, nothing was impossible. Even though I was still learning who He was, I knew that together, it could be accomplished.

*For being a newer Christ follower, I had such determination to follow Him and knew without a doubt that He would come through for me. *

With the benefit being exactly one month away, I had no time to waste. I marched into work the following day, ready to work my shift when I saw my manager, Jordan, sitting at the wooden desk.

All full of excitement, I exclaimed, "I am going to buy the satin A-line Mikaela dress this month. Can you please please please not sell it off the rack?"

With confusion, Jordan proceeded with the same line of questioning as my mom, "You're going to do what? Why?"

After answering Jordan's questions the best I could, I pushed the envelope by asking her not only to avoid selling that gown to anyone else, but also to sell it to me at a discounted price, knowing it was a sample. Jordan thought for a second, agreed to my terms and gave me a 10% discount.

Great, I thought! I was off to a fantastic start! If God gave me this task, surely, He is going to make sure I see it through, I concluded.

*It's funny how it was such a large bill (literally), but there was no moment of doubt in my mind...wonder what that was all about. *

I worked in a ritzy town, which was one of the most expensive areas in the Twin Cities. There was an outdoor shopping area where I worked so I took the opportunity, while the shop was covered, to walk over to the local boutiques to speak to the owners.

I went to a jewelry store where I knew the owners well and explained my predicament. I asked for any donations they would be willing to chip in to make Tanya's dream a reality. The jewelry store owner looked taken back but also like she wanted to be a part of a larger story, and with that, she handed me $100. With this new boost of confidence, I decided to continue to the stores where I knew the owners to plead the same case. After a few more shops added to Tanya's cause, I found it best to head back to work, whilst I still had a job to return to.

In the evening, Jordan had left and Susana had come in. Susana was a woman in her seventies, originally from New York, who was the shop's seamstress. Susana was a whole 4'8 of sass with a mop of black hair and a full outlook on life. I loved working with Susana. She had seen so much and always shared about her crazy New York parties, her trips to the Caymans, and her rich husband's estate.

As we were catching up, I proceeded to tell her all about the two brides I met the day before and what my mission was. Susana laughed, not sure if this was because of my naivety or because she liked a woman who could handle a challenge, and added, "I'll give her a discounted rate on her alterations."

Knowing that we were taking a bridal size 10 off the rack and would have to make it into a street size 4 was a large and unrecommended task, but Susana was a natural and she knew she would be up to the challenge. I formally had us type up the information with the discount she was offering and had her initial the page. Not knowing what I was going to do with this piece of paper, I stored it into a folder and finished my shift, thrilled with the day's progress.

As I headed home, my head was flooding with ideas about how I was going to raise the rest of the money and if I should include Tanya or Sandra into this plan.

Now at home, I jumped on my computer, went to Facebook, and scrolled to the twins. I decided the best thing to do was message Sandra to tell her about what I was planning on doing and to get permission out of respect for her family.

Typing in the message, I thought, "Man, I might come across totally crazy right now, but here goes nothing." I hit enter and moments later, watched as someone was typing on the other end of the screen.

Sandra typed something along the effect of, "That is the nicest thing I have ever heard! You absolutely have my blessing!"

I shared with her my plan to have the wedding dress in tow with me at her benefit, as a complete surprise to Tanya. I asked for her not to say anything to Tanya and proceed like normal when she saw me at the benefit. We said our goodbyes and promised we would see each other in a little less than a month.

*Okay, the pressure's on, I thought. There's no going back! *

While on Facebook, I created an event, telling the whole story of who Tanya was, why this was important, and the goal. I shared it with all my friends and friends. Through friends' generosity, they helped donate a few hundred dollars! I signed off and called my little sister on the phone.

"Hey Ally. Are you busy? No? Okay, I'm coming over. You're going to help me!" And with that, I drove over to see my baby sis.

My little sister Ally is always up for spending time with her older sisters. Whether it's us poking fun at her or just being involved in the same activity, Ally just wants to be included.

Being nine years younger than me, I thought that using Ally's adorable innocence could really come in handy. I drove to my mom's house in the suburbs, found Ally watching *Army Wives* in the basement, and told her all about what had happened to me a few days before. I explained that we were both going door-to-door around the neighborhood to collect donations for Tanya's dress. I needed her as the cute, innocent factor and as a source of credibility in what we were doing, but also as my comfort blanket if this plan failed epically. Reluctantly, she came along with the stipulation that she wasn't going to say anything and I'd owe her Chipotle.

We started easy by going down our block with familiar faces. At this point, I had learned how to give the "Tanya pitch" in a few short sentences.

With the utmost passion, I would say something to the effect, "Hi there. This is Ally and I'm Erica. We're out here today asking for your donation for a sweet girl named Tanya. You see, I work at a bridal salon and recently, I met Tanya. Tanya wasn't like most brides I see; Tanya was dealing with a life-threatening disease, all while just going through thyroid cancer and recently given birth. She is not well and is fearful she won't make it to her wedding day. But when she tried on this wedding dress, everything changed. She lit up and for the first time, she could see herself getting married. We're here today trying to raise money to buy her that wedding dress, so we can present it to her at her medical benefit. Would you be willing to donate for this cause?"

This sparked a lot of interesting conversations and new interactions with nearby neighbors. Hours later, Ally and I walked away with our heads held high as we raised a few hundred dollars. Score!

*Man, God, you sure want this plan to happen, huh? *

With only a few weeks left, I was wondering what else I could do to raise money and help. Being that I worked in the bridal industry, I thought to call up my vendor friends; florists, photographers, and venues to see if they would donate money or their services at a reduced cost. To my surprise, many obliged, and I ended up with a thick folder of discounts and freebies to present to Tanya on the day of her benefit, which was completely unexpected and quite frankly, an afterthought.

In the final days leading up to her benefit, I was still a bit short with the funds. But like Jesus-clockwork, I went downstairs to check the mailbox, and wouldn't you know, my taxes were sitting right there. I tore open the white envelope and I kid you not, it was the exact amount of money that was left to buy the wedding dress.

I rushed to the bank right away, cashed the check, and added it to my thick stash of cash for Tanya's fund.

*The money was the exact amount that I needed to pay the dress off...WHAT?! God, you seriously think about all the tiny details! *

With two days to spare, I went to the bridal shop I was working at, found Jordan, handed her the plump envelope with a huge smile, and said, "I did it! I can finally give her the Mikaela wedding dress!"

Jordan was blown away that I pulled it off, and in such a short amount of time. She helped me take the dress down off the rack and put it into an oversized bridal bag, and with that, I rushed it back home.

****

Waking up the morning of Tanya's benefit, I was filled with more nerves than a skydiver on a windy day. The day was upon me and it was becoming so real. The emotions of what the day was going to hold and how her life was going to be changed in a moment was overwhelming for me. I was shaking from it all. I curled my hair, put on my grey peplum top and black dangle earrings, and out the door I went. The GPS said it was going to take an hour and fifteen minutes, so during that time, I prayed.

Lord, give me strength. Help me have the right words to say when the moment comes. I am so nervous over how she's going to react. I pray, Lord God, that this would be well received and viewed solely as a gift from you. I don't know your plan for all of this, but you do, and I trust you. Thank you, Lord, for letting me be a part of a larger story. Amen.

****

As I was pulling up, I noticed a swarm of people heading into the large auditorium to be a part of the benefit festivities.

I left the dress along with the blue vinyl folder in the car and headed inside, acting as casual as I possibly could, though I imagine my face was flushed red with a shiny forehead from all the nervous grease.

I surveyed the benefit, seeing what these things were all about, as this was the first I had ever been to. Tanya really did it right; there was an auction, live music, a cash bar, buffet, donation stops everywhere you went, and close to 500 people in attendance.

As I didn't know anyone and I went by myself, I hopped from different station to station, chatting with people as I went.

When I met someone new, they would ask, "How do you know Tanya?" and I would chuckle, "Oh, I met her and Sandra last month at the bridal store I work at. We all just hit it off and they invited me, so here I am."

Within a few minutes of mingling, I spotted Tanya. Tanya looked beautiful with her golden locks, stylish black and white dress, and pink lip balm. I loved her smile because it was so genuine and rare and when she did it, it lit up the room. Tanya wasn't one who liked all the attention; she liked being tucked into the background, so I could tell sense that she was uncomfortable with having all eyes on her.

Tanya came towards me with the biggest smile and exclaimed, "I can't believe you're here! I didn't think you were actually going to come!"

"Of course, I came! I wouldn't have missed it for the world!"

Dazzled, Tanya locked arms with me and introduced me to a bunch of her friends.

"This is Erica. She is fabulous and works at that bridal salon I was telling you about. Have you met Erica? She's fabulous and single!"

Being in her presence made me feel like I was the guest of honor! In that moment, she made me feel like I was the only person she cared to show up, like I was her long-lost best friend who she hadn't seen in a century. My secretive nerves were quickly turning from a nervous energy to a calm tranquil vibe, all thanks to her.

*Thank you, Jesus, for answering that prayer! But also, why was I such a big deal to her? *

After what felt like the "Erica social," I told her I was going to head to the bathroom, but really, I had different plans. I had spotted Sandra in her bright jumpsuit from the corner of my eye and beelined straight to her. Jumping up and down, we hugged, knowing that I had dual purposes for being there. She shrieked, "Do you have it?!"

With mellowed tones, as to not blow our cover, I whispered back, "Yes, I do! It's in my car. When should I get it?"

Sandra quickly formulated a plan and told me to go to my car, grab the dress, and wait outside of the building. She would make up a reason for Tanya, and her mom, to head outside with her to find me.

I walked briskly to my car, feeling like my nerves had come back but this time, with an army. Tanya had no idea what was about to happen. I quickly hustled with my shiny folder and dress bag off to the right of the building.

As I was waiting, word must have spread because more and more people were finding their way outside. Friends of the family, friends of friends, female, male, young and old were staring at me with smiles and laughter as to what was about to happen in mere moments, still unbeknownst to Tanya. I saw Sandra take a step out of the door and I knew Tanya was just milliseconds behind her.

I could hear Tanya saying, "What's going on? What did you have to tell me?"

As soon as she got out that last question, Tanya pivoted and made eye contact with me. Her hands cupped her mouth, and her eyes became watery as she passed her sister and beelined straight towards me. Both of us paced towards each other with tears filling our eyes and the dress bag held over my head. We met in the middle and embraced each other with tears.

Tanya paused and through her tears spewed out, "I don't understand. What's going on?"

As I opened my mouth, the words bounced into the air, "This is God's way of letting you know that you are going to make it to your wedding day. This is yours."

*I had absolutely no idea I was going to say that or what God's intentions were until He spoke through me. Another answered prayer. *

Tears of joy streaming down both of our faces, we embraced each other for what felt like the whole afternoon. I handed her the white cotton dress bag and as she was starting to unzip it, you could tell she was hesitantly opening it like a plastic snake was going to bounce out.

She unzipped the bag to find her dream A-line Mikaela dress. She gave me another tight hug, showing how she felt in this moment because there were no more words. I handed her the thick folder and told her to look at it later.

We walked together to put everything in her car, she embraced me again and said, "Thank you Erica. Thank you so much. We knew from the moment we met you that you were an angel. Now it's confirmed."

*They felt something about me? An angel? It's incredible to hear that someone else felt that nudge from God, and that this time, it was about me. *

I ran to my car to fix my black smeared liquid eyeliner before heading back into the party. Trying to transition back into her event, I continued mingling, eating short ribs from the buffet, and playing coin toss games that were set out.

By this time, word had completely spread, and I was now known as "the girl who gave Tanya her wedding dress." But Tanya and I both knew I was more than that to her; I was God's messenger.

* *

Fast forward one year later. As the most beautiful bride, Tanya walked down the aisle with her little girl in tow, to the love of her life. I was honored to be apart of her bridal party and get to know her friends and family on a closer level.

One year later, Tanya was my best friend. One year later, Tanya's faith had been restored. One year later, Tanya's symptoms significantly improved. One year later, Tanya continued to expand her family, when she was told she would never have more than one baby.

Side Note: It was only through God's power that I was able to raise that amount of money. It was only through God's power that I was able to have the confidence to go door-to-door, ask for donations, and use my own earnings. It was only through His power was I able to use the skills He has given me to use for the greater good. I couldn't have been able to do any of that without God. Instead, I listened to the Holy Spirit, took the ultimate leap of faith by believing that voice above anyone else's.

It wasn't me who spoke those words when I gave that dress to her. When I started out on the journey of getting her that dress, I didn't know all that God was doing. I didn't know that at the time, Tanya had lost her way from God and that all she could hear was the enemy. I didn't know that she felt that God had forgotten about her and was angry that God wasn't stopping all the pain she was enduring. I didn't know that the wedding dress was a symbol of new life. I didn't know that a wonderful friendship based on faith was being born. All I knew was that if I dove in headfirst to what felt like the right step, God would bless me for being obedient to those "feelings," aka the Holy Spirit.

While this testimony was incredibly life changing for me, just think about what it meant for Tanya. Tanya had felt that she couldn't hear or see God. Tanya had cried out to God but through all her own suffering, she couldn't see past the darkness. The enemy had held her captive as his own. But the Lord God does not give up on His children.

It says in *Ephesians 6:12, "for our struggle is not against flesh and blood, but against the rulers, against the authorities, against the powers of this dark world and against the spiritual forces of evil in the heavenly realms."

God reinstated her faith and said, "Tanya, I'm here. I've been here. Don't give up because I haven't." And just like that, I (a very small piece) was used in the much larger picture of restoring a faith or many faiths that day and God gets all the glory!!

Past Tanya and myself, think about the ripple effect this story might have had on Sandra, their mom, the guests at the benefit, the nice people whose doors got knocked on, the shop manager, and maybe even you right now as you read these words. God wants to touch each one of us with His movement. He wants every single one of His creations to know that He is working in our lives and it is possible for you to have the same type of experience, growing closer to God.

These small "coincidences" are God's way of trying to speak to you. Are you hearing Him, or are you brushing it off as "Wow, that was funny how I just ran into so-and-so," or "I can't believe they just paid for our meal, especially while we were struggling to pay for it."

If you are reading this right now and you believe God doesn't care about you or He doesn't actively come after you like a thirsty third date, you are mistaken, my friend!

Praise our Holy God who can make all things happen in His name! Realize that each and every talent, passion, and skill you have was purposely selected for you to have; but, not without a cost. When He calls upon you, be ready to use it! It's a great honor to be used in that way and really, it is our duty!

God is incredibly good. We may not know why He calls us to do certain things, but if He calls, be ready to pick up that receiver. God is all-knowing and knew the intricate web that was Tanya, and it took a complete outsider with the skills God had given her to be able to revive her faith. Amen to that.

*NLT version

Life's Transitions

At this point, I was weeks away from graduating from my community college with an associate in arts degree, and still didn't have a grip on the actual job that I wanted. About as quickly as I thought about it, an advertisement popped up on my computer screen that was meant for me.

*What a coincidence...! *

It was an advertisement for a wedding planning institute. From the moment I saw it, I knew this was my next step. This school taught all about the wedding industry, how to run your own wedding planning firm, and the steps of planning a wedding. I was instantly hooked. I researched all my options of how I would pay for this trade school and where I would attend the classes, and like instant Jesus-ramen, it all fell into place. Within one month, I was attending classes online and paid for my schooling in cash from the waitressing jobs I had throughout college, alongside my bridal job. I had never felt more alive and in charge of my future.

*It's obvious this is what God wants for me, otherwise, why would it have popped up in front of me at this exact moment? *

The wedding planning institute was everything I had hoped it would have been and more. This eight-month course taught all aspects of the wedding industry ranging from diamonds, dress types, venues, wedding showers, and so on.

Not only did I learn extensively about the industry I had fallen into and adored, the course also taught how to open and manage your own bridal shop. Because my parents both owned their own companies, I had mixed thoughts about being an entrepreneur, but I loved the knowledge this trade school taught, either way.

A month after completing my wedding certificate, I enrolled in a 4-year university. I wasn't overly enthused about this particular university because I really had my heart set on an art school. Nevertheless, I had committed to staying on my fashion path.

I had known that a Communications degree was something I was really interested in too, so I decided to study both. I've always excelled at all things communication and writing, so I figured this would be a good route for me as well as, transferrable in a multitude of career paths.

That fall, I turned into a full-time student in Communications with an emphasis in Journalism and minoring in fashion studies. I soaked up the information like a sponge and felt that somehow, these classes at the university would benefit me greatly.

With my communication courses, I really enjoyed taking classes like non-verbal communication, public speaking, interpersonal and intercultural relations courses, and I excelled at them, which made the journey even better. Because my major was so broad, I had an emphasis in journalism where a huge part of what I did throughout college was write essay papers and other types of writing pieces. I can't express to you how much I adored doing them.

With my fashion courses, though, it wasn't panning out quite how I was thinking. The courses either pointed you towards design or buying. Alongside my incredibly talented wanna-be-*Project Runway* classmates, I was feeling insecure with my own physical abilities to draw, sew, or design. And I really didn't excel on the buying side due to my lack of math abilities. But regardless, I was hoping that over time, I would find my fashion calling.

Alongside being a student, I was still working part-time as a food server and bridal consultant. I shifted bridal companies and ended up at a vintage bridal shop, selling gowns from the 1900-early 2000s. The job at the vintage bridal gowns only lasted for a short while. I was extremely grateful for the opportunity to work there, especially because while I was studying history of costume design at the university, I was actually seeing different time piece silhouettes in real time.

Ultimately, I felt underutilized, like my ideas and strengths weren't being taken advantage of. I would feel the fabrics and study the dresses all day long, but the opportunity to sell them was never on the table, so, I felt I had to move on.

I always had waitressing as my good and faithful, though. Waitressing came naturally, and it was such a fun way for me to meet others. Waitressing was also a relief from my everyday school life. I enjoyed it very much and more than that, I noticed that I really excelled at it based on the feedback I received from customers, management, and my reflected tips. And even though I loved waitressing, I still wanted to get back into selling bridal dresses, especially if I wanted to be ready for NYC.

Getting done with my afternoon classes, I headed to the library to unwind on the computer through mindlessly scrolling social media. I opened the tab to LinkedIn to peek at job titles that interested me and even more, figuring out if those types of jobs would be available in New York.

This was all happening in 2014 when Kleinfelds, or *Say Yes to The Dress* was the popular and well-known binge worthy reality show. Everyone who watched television knew about this show and it's prestigious reputation.

While I was on LinkedIn, I was hunting around different bridal companies, including Kleinfelds, to see which employees I could connect with. Feeling courageous, I reached out to members of Kleinfelds' staff to connect with me. But I felt it on my heart to take it another step further.

*Hmmmm…. Where does this ballsy confidence come from? *

I asked the owner to be my connection. Then I thought, what harm is there in private messaging her? So, I did.

Side note: If my mom has taught me one thing in my life, it is, "Walk into every room like you own it!"

Quivering, I clicked on Mara's profile, found the message button, and hit send, then proceeded on with my cultural norms essay.

Within Jesus-time minutes, a notification popped up on my screen saying that Mara Ursel sent me a message. I didn't just jump out of my chair, I leaped! Mara was thanking me for my kind words and asked me to send my resume for consideration for their current bridal consultant position.

I was so over the moon with excitement that I called my dad and stepmom, Beth, right away and said, "You guys! Can you help me get my resume looking New York ready? I'm sending it to someone very important!"

Early the next morning, I received the final approved version and hit the send button to Mara. I was shaken by the mere fact that this New York fashionista would be interested in a Midwestern gal who hardly had any experience in comparison to those hot shot New Yorkers.

Hours later, back in intercultural relations class, the teacher was going on and on about the importance of recognizing non-verbal cues when I received a phone call from a New York number. Getting glares from my other classmates, I stepped out of class, jittery with who could be on the other line. I answered the phone and was monotonality greeted by Mara's secretary.

"Hello, it's Denise, Mara Ursel's secretary. We would like you to come in for an interview. When works for you?"

A true New Yorker with her dry and right to the point way, I shuffled quickly through my planner to see when I could sneak away.

"Oh my gosh! Thank you so much for calling me and giving me the opportunity. Ahhh, will the, um, 23rd work?"

"Sure. I'll put you down for 11am. We'll see you then." Click.

My mind was blown! Why would the largest wedding dress store and in New York of all places be interested in a nobody Minnesotan like me? I wondered.

I set up an interview for exactly three weeks later and didn't even have time to put two and two together at how little time away that really was. Literally pacing through the common area and showing more teeth than Julia Roberts, I quickly dialed my mom.

"Mom!!! Pack your bags! We're going to New York!"

Neither my mom nor I had ever been to New York. The most we knew about New York was what we saw on tv. But my mom and I are alike in a lot of ways...we are both spontaneous and love adventure, so, I knew there wouldn't have been anyone better than her to go on this once in a lifetime kind of trip together.

Weeks later, we jetted off to New York so I could be interviewed by Kleinfelds. My inspiration for my look was Carrie Bradshaw: Think curly blonde hair, a daring, yet professional two-toned pink and black dress, and bright satin lips.

Mom hung around the coffee shop around the corner while I strolled into the beautiful store on Sixth Ave. I spoke to the front desk coordinator, told her about my interview at eleven, and was told to sit in the plush seated waiting room. My eyes couldn't stay still as I darted at the beautifully dressed mannequins, phenomenal wedding dresses with sparkles and sequins, and of course, gorgeous women.

Moments later, Sara from the TV show had said her hellos and escorted me to a room. Sara was very friendly, always with a smile, making me feel very comfortable, while talking casually to me about my experiences thus far in New York. She was wondering why I had applied for the job and why I believed I would be a right fit for the company. After minutes speaking together, Sara left the room.

Ten more people came in and out of the room to interview me, many of which I had seen on the show. After my last interview, I asked if I could get a tour (my motto is "there is no harm in trying!") and they happily obliged.

The store was so beautifully organized and much larger than I had originally thought based on the show. Even their collections of gowns were unlike anything I have ever seen in Minnesota. Shades of pinks, blues, Chantilly lace, and corsets were enough to convince me this was the place for me.

The last stop on the tour was to visit Mara's office. I made sure to thank her over and over for the experience and the opportunity, then glided out of Kleinfelds over an hour later.

It was a cloud nine type of experience. After that trip, I was even more determined to be living in New York, especially now that I had seen it in person.

My mom and I stayed for a long weekend and did all the tourist things like seeing the Statue of Liberty, Rockefeller Center, One World Trade Center, *Chicago* on Broadway, and of course, we ordered a few Cosmo's as an homage to Ms. Bradshaw. Both of us had the time of our lives while we acted like two single girls in the streets of Manhattan with our newly owned fake Prada bags. I knew from the moment I stepped into those crowded streets that it wasn't a coincidence that I was there. My confidence hailing for taxis and fast walking only confirmed that New York was meant to be my next home.

*Having such high confidence was something I was no stranger to, but now it was starting to click why… *

Jumping back into my collegiate schedule, I was sitting in my introduction to film class, walking all my eager friends through the details of the trip, when I received a phone call from a New York number.

Denise, aka Canada dry, was on the other line, thanking me for coming in but let me know that they were going to hire someone else for the position. I let out a quick sigh and before I could say more, she continued by saying that sixteen girls were fighting for the same position so I shouldn't take it personally.

I interjected by asking, "Is there a particular reason I didn't get selected?"

Denise shortly responded, "You are so nice. We may be worried that you can't handle the harsh personalities here."

Well thanks, Minnesota Nice! Though I was bummed by their decision, it was short lived. I knew in my heart of hearts that the timing wasn't right. I was a junior in college and wasn't interested in dropping out or transferring into a new school for only a year. I just wanted to remember their feedback and move forward, knowing that I was on fire for New York after that trip, and excited that the possibility was alive.

*It's so funny seeing how God works. He put the desire on my heart to want to move to New York through *Sex and The City* at such a young age. He gave me the desire to be a part of fashion, which specifically led to bridal. From there, He showed me that there were options and opportunities in New York, specifically with sales. God is simply the coolest! *

Side Note: The way I handled the rejection, in one ear and out the other, made the world of difference. I didn't dwell on the fact that I didn't get the position, but rather, that gave me a sneak peek into what I could have and made me hungrier for the New York life. It also let me know that next time I interviewed in New York to come with a thicker skin, or at least the perception of one.

Setbacks aren't failures. Opportunities can be presented to you that you think are perfect for you, but then they won't work out.

Don't think of it as a failure because it didn't pan out. It's a win because you got to view the opportunity in the first place. God will open doors and close doors that align with what is best for you. If a door closes, know that it could be because there is a better one waiting. As cliché sounding as it is, God's dream is way bigger than what you could have possibly wanted in the first place.

With Kleinfelds, that was simply a door God wanted to show me but not ultimately give me.

My Future Called Me

When I got back home, I had that fire within me to hop back into bridal. I went to the largest and most acclaimed bridal store in the Twin Cities and applied (with Kleinfelds predominantly listed on my resume as an experience). Within one day, I got called back for an interview for the bridal consultant position.

With Dry Canada's feedback in mind, I had this new cocky, know it all persona. During the interview, I bragged about my Kleinfeld interview, my past bridal experiences, that I study fashion in college, and outpoured my passion of the industry. Instantly, they hired me.

*Coincidence that with all three bridal positions, I got hired on the spot? I think not! *

At my new bridal job, I was hungry, wanting to soak in everything I could. I got an opportunity to tour their bridal warehouse and calling center, which gave me a different insight into the business.

I got to speak one-on-one with a wholesale representative from Mori Lee bridal.

I became very familiar with each designer's style and price point, and I learned how to perfectly accessorize them. I loved working at this company, but there were some things that I wasn't feeling rewarded with.

After seeing Kleinfeld's selection, I was feeling like what we carried in Minnesota was so bland in comparison, and it didn't give me the same fire as the dresses in New York. I often told co-workers that the dresses were so vanilla in comparison. (You can see there was a real diva personality on the rise.)

Even in my free time, I would study bridal magazines. It was important for me to know the newest bridal trends in gowns and accessories. I kept up to date with the newest silhouettes, color palettes, and upcoming designers. I made an inspirational journal where I would cut out pictures from bridal magazines that I found innovative and fresh, then paste them into my journal. This soon was my newest hobby that became a fun creative outlet, that is until my next hobby came along.

I was always looking around for the next thing for me to get into. I was wanting to find a program with meaning that I could be involved in. And that's when a Jesus-sized ton of bricks fell into my lap, and I found *Operation Glass Slipper*.

Operation Glass Slipper was a non-profit organization that helps high school girls get prom dresses, accessories, and alterations for no cost, when they themselves do not have a budget or the means to get these things. I dove right into this idea.

I volunteered at the event as a "Fairy Godmother" one May at the local mall and was hooked! A Fairy Godmother would assist girls by finding the perfect dress, accessories, and then repeat. I absolutely loved doing this. Not only was it the identical task of the job I loved, but it changed these girls lives, which was just an added bonus.

While I had a lunch break, I went around trying to find the owner so I could see how I could become even more involved.

Pam, with her hair tucked above her ears and round glasses, was the sweetest lady you could ever met. She was loveable and always had a smile from ear to ear, even if she was in the middle of chaos. Pam quickly said she would love help in her warehouse during the week and gave me her contact information. That night, I emailed Pam asking if I could come that same week to help, and she was over the moon! I ended up going to her warehouse once a week to help with whatever she needed. In the warehouse, we would organize, tag, bag, separate, and move around dresses to better prepare for the next event.

Pam quickly became a mentor to me because she knew a lot about the bridal and fashion industry, as she had worked in it for over half her life. I loved hanging out with Pam because she knew the gossip in the industry and I believe, loved the fact that someone admired her non-profit the way I did.

I asked how she started her business, where she got funded, how she made connections, and a million other questions because I was hungry to know. To me, Pam had the dream job. She was actually making a difference in the community. She was doing God's work and through it all, was the happiest woman I'd ever met (alongside my stepmom Beth). Pam and I quickly became very close, knowing all the ins and outs of our lives and especially, knowing that I was starving for more.

*I had no idea that working for God was an option, until I met Pam. Is it possible to do both? I couldn't get the idea out of my head. *

One weekday while I was helping in the warehouse, I spotted three racks of bridal gowns pushed in the back corner of this large box space. Typically, I only saw prom dresses, so you better believe that once I saw those bridal gowns, my eyes popped out of my head like a cartoon character.

Instantly, I skipped over to examine the dresses to feel the fabric. Before I could even formulate a plan, I asked Pam, "Hey, what are you doing with all of these dresses?"

Pam had said that with all the donations, sometimes wedding dresses got thrown in with them. When she gets a surplus of them, she will host one event to get rid of the bridal gowns. Until then, they just sat in her warehouse.

With no time for my brain to think, I sputtered, "Well, what if I take them, try to sell them, and we'll split the profit?"

Pam raised her right eyebrow, looking very impressed, and got up from her chair, saying, "Okay. Well, here's how we should do it then."

Pam was always a great supporter and played along with my dreams. She listened to my wacky ideas and brainstormed with me how to make them happen.

I got right to it and grabbed the twenty-two dresses she had, put them into bags, labeled them by their popularity, and put them into the trunk of my car. I took the bridal gowns to my 700 square foot one-bedroom space, put them into my miniature walk-in closet, and planned to sell them online. This is when *Couture on the Go* was born.

Couture on the Go was an online e-commerce business where brides could buy these gently used bridal gowns at a fraction of the cost of regular retail. This venture was so fun for me because I got to create a business exactly how I wanted to and use my knowledge of how I had seen other bridal salons work, alongside what I was taught from The Wedding Planning Institute. It was like it was all coming together.

*Well, that's interesting (she says while trying to piece together the puzzle). *

Still being a college student, *Couture on the Go* was a fun hobby of mine. With all my creative ideas and online efforts, truth be told, it never really took off. Instead, I was the crazy girl with twenty-two wedding dresses in my closet for over four years. Hello crazy, my name is Erica. But even after four years, I didn't want to give up; I knew somehow there was a greater plan at play.

*Where do all of these strong instincts come from? *

Now at this point in the story, I was close to finishing college. I was taking theology classes, attending church weekly by myself, and trying to figure out how I felt about faith, God, and The Trinity, outside of what my parents had told me. I had a new set of eyes on, which was as child-like as possible, starting from scratch.

I had never been baptized, gone to Sunday school, or even read the Bible. In fact, I was feeling quite inadequate because I didn't know much, scripturally.

Why is a man named Jonah in a fish? Who's walking on water? There were how many disciples? But I was parched, and I knew only God could quench my thirst. I wanted to go on this self-discovery journey, and a contemporary church in the Twin Cities is the exact place I found it.

Entrepreneur Time

At this stage in my life, I had just broken up with yet another boyfriend. I had dated Lucas for three years. Lucas was charming, rebellious, and handsome in a punk rock kind of way. Ultimately, the bad boy that you don't end up marrying.

I knew God had big dreams for me to travel and make something out of my life. Lucas, on the other hand, was very content staying in the same town we grew up in, not finishing college, and hanging around the same type of people. In the end, I needed more for myself and believed that God had someone in store for me. I threw my hat in the ring and was ready to fully trust that God would do the searching for me. I said a prayer to God and decided to give up the topic of my love life.

God, please forgive me. I have been pretending to be you for all these years, trying to find my other half, and quite frankly, I've done a terrible job. I'm sorry that I didn't trust you. I'm sorry that I showed no patience. Lord, I'm done. I'm done trying. I'm done playing mind games and wasting thoughts on when he's going to call or whether I said the thing he wanted to hear. Lord, I'm done searching. I leave this topic right here and right now. I will wait patiently until you reveal who my husband is going to be, if that's even your plan. Thank you, Lord. I love you and I thank you for taking this burden off my shoulders. Amen.

* *

I was in my third year of college and desperately wanting to focus on myself and what was best for me. After the breakup, I also needed somewhere to live and to find a roommate. After talking with my best friend, Olivia, of over ten years, she told me that a co-worker of hers was also looking for a place to live in the city. Just like that, the shenanigans of Erica and Laura began.

I had met Laura a few times in passing and group outings, but we never focused on getting to know each other individually. Once we both heard that we were looking for roommates in the Twin Cities, we knew this would be a good match.

We met up for some margaritas to discuss what we were looking for and instantly clicked. We were both being newly single, ready to be independent and excited to explore things that other single, twenty-year olds were doing. I did go through the party college student phase, but during all of this, my relationship with God was really flourishing.

He wasn't so distant anymore. I spoke to Jesus every day just like my big brother and likewise, I heard from Him. I kept my eyes and ears open for what the next big thing was, hoping to be used again, like I was with Tanya.

While I was having the time of my life with Laura, I could tell that this phase was also destructive. Going out and partying all the time is the gateway that could have led me down the wrong path. It felt like I had two sides of me; the Erica from church who was hungry for God and the single, fun Erica who loved Syrah. The Holy Spirit was pulling me closer to Him, while the enemy was saying, "Come on, one more drink!"

But the enemy had already lost the war, and I knew he wasn't going to win this battle either. Around this time, God sent me an angel named Fatima, exactly when I needed her.

Now that Laura and I were living in our new house in the cities and getting settled, I was driving around trying to better understand the neighborhood.

I came across a Wells Fargo, which was perfect because I had that on my list of errands for the day. Walking into this unfamiliar bank location, I saw right away that there was a wide mix of ethnicities, with me being the minority white girl. This was a new experience, as I came from a very white suburban setting, always a majority race. Living in the city was completely different. White, black, Hispanic, Asian, it all blended. It was like a gorgeous rainbow piñata. Going to this Wells Fargo was just the tip of it.

I stepped up to the podium to announce that I would like to speak with a banker. I wanted to meet with a banker to go over some financial goals I had with *Couture on the Go*. I got called to sit down with this beautiful ebony skinned woman named Fatima.

Instantly, I was drawn to her. Fatima had this glow about her, something very childlike and non-judgmental that made you want to know more about her. Fatima started the conversation by asking what brought me in and how she could help, but somehow our conversation changed quickly from ranking in the monopoly for *Couture on the Go* to who we were as people. I started telling Fatima about what I did, what this business was about, and quickly learned through the process that she was interested in both me and the business.

Fatima was a native African from The Gambia who had moved to the U.S. ten years ago with her two kids. She was a curious woman, always wanting to learn more about life and other people's ways. She explained to me that life in Gambia didn't have these westernized wedding gowns and if they did, they were not easily achievable to get because of the price and the distance to travel to get to them.

Pretty quickly, our talk morphed into taking *Couture on the Go* to Africa for a month-long bridal pop-up shop, getting rid of all my inventory; and if all went well, we would continue the same pattern.

*God had to have orchestrated us meeting because it was too much of a coincidence that she was so interested in me. *

From that day forward, we exchanged numbers and set a date to talk further about our vision.

Meeting at random Starbucks locations a few times a month, we would discuss how we would transport the inventory, where we would get the displays, how we were going to market the business, and showed our everlasting commitment to this new project.

Showing my sincerity, I had submitted for a tourist visa, preparing for our departure. While the first few meetings were business heavy, we started transitioning into personal details of our lives until we became very close friends.

I started going over to her house to meet her children, Ameena and Mohamed, whom I adored very much, and they would come over for breakfast. I would take her kids to the library until she finished up work, then join them for dinner. We were more than potential business partners; we were becoming the best of friends.

At this point, both sets of my parents all knew about *Couture on the Go*, Fatima, and my dreams of moving to New York. Beth, my stepmom, who had really come to be the most supportive woman in my life, happened to also be my greatest spiritual mentor. Once Beth knew about our plans to take *Couture on the Go* to Africa, she decided that she needed to meet the woman I was planning on leaving the country with.

With an innocent and non-judgmental heart, Beth came down to Wells Fargo with me, ready to learn more about Fatima. Beth asked hard questions that I hadn't even thought to ask like, "What was your childhood like, where did you graduate from, and what are your thoughts on God?"

I leaned in hard to hear that last question, like someone reaching for the last spring roll, waiting on what Fatima was going to say. She proceeded to answer that she is Muslim and about 90% of Gambia is too.

As quickly as those words came out of Fatima's mouth, the same lightbulb that popped over my head before, had re-appeared. At that moment, God had shared with me the bigger picture as to why I was doing this. Yes, I was going to help women get wedding gowns at a low price, but also, I was there to show the power of Christ's love and compassion through the program. And just like that, both Beth and I walked away from that outing knowing exactly what the grand scheme was.

*How incredible is God? The way He orchestrates relationships, long before we even know the plan behind it?! Also, what a weird coincidence that I went into my bank and worked with that particular banker! *

The coolest part of our friendship, though, has been watching her faith grow in Christ. When I met Fatima, she was Muslim. This was exciting because it meant that I had the chance to talk about God and make Fatima my actual sister in Christ. But I was never pushy.

When we first met at the bank, I told her right away about my faith because it is a part of who I am and how I saw myself running my business. When we had that initial business meeting at Starbucks, I talked about how we should incorporate God into our business model and that He is the reason we are doing this.

Never once did I shy away or hide what my intentions were with my own relationship with God or my own plan for *Couture on the Go*. Once I started to get to know her more personally and met her two kids, I again spoke about my faith. Fatima would always say that there was something about me, some light in my face and positivity that she loved.

Always, I would chuckle, "That's God seeping through me, Christ who is living in me. You can have that too..."

Throughout our relationship, I have seen her become more and more curious about God. One time, she asked about my church and the next week, she went to church with me. Then, she asked a question about God and I answered it to the best of my abilities. One evening as I strolled into Fatima's house, I stepped into the doorway she said, "Erica, guess where I was last night? A Christian concert! I loved it!"

That was music to my ears! Teaching someone about God is as simple as showing them yourself, and that is exactly what our relationship was. What she initially noticed about me came from The Holy Spirit and just explaining why that was there and what that means, better explains who God is.

I never pushed because I could see that God was working on her heart, slowly and surely. I was just happy to be that vessel in the larger picture.

*God removed any stigmas I may have had with talking about Him to a non-Christian. Isn't that beautiful?

* *

Unfortunately, *Couture on the Go* never got up and running. And that is just how things work sometimes. Even when God puts things in your path, it doesn't always mean it is meant to last, but rather, there may have been a whole different reason for it.

Think of a time when you had a good friend but over time, you broke off your friendship. The reality is that everything has a purpose for why it enters into your story and the time frame attached. That is what *Couture on the Go* and the idea of moving it to Africa was, a beautiful idea, ultimately pointing someone to Christ. Fatima and I are still great friends and still day dream of going to The Gambia together, one day.

Seeing Clearly

Let me tell you a gorgeous gift I have been given. I dream vivid, realistic dreams that are direct messages from God. Sounds pretty cool, huh? Let me tell you about one of them.

In this particular dream, I could see things from a third person perspective, almost like how you view things in a shooter game. I was walking outside on an uneven, chalky beige road with the sun beaming down on me. The roads were surrounded by beautiful people, all with long black hair and dark skin, wandering the streets, with street carts lining the background.

There was one woman who stood out to me, as she was the focus of the dream. Everyone else in the dream was moving, but she was standing in the middle of the road wearing an all-red sari, as beautiful as a caramel skinned Barbie. I only saw her from her profile, but she had a posture and stance that was mesmerizing. And that was it. The dream only lasted what seemed like seven seconds. There was no speaking and no interaction; just observation from my third person perspective.

* *

I had been attending my new church for about six months. I loved it for many reasons. One reason was because I felt this was a church where I could learn the basics and then after each message, dive into my own notes through research.

I had really gotten into the groove of the church by attending volunteer events, making friends, and becoming a member of the congregation, being a greeter, helping at food drives, and becoming known.

I attended all the classes the church offered, like *Alpha* and *Financial Peace University*, soaking in this newfound knowledge I so badly craved. I was happy with how I was progressing but was ready for the next thing God had in store for me.

The following Sunday morning, I was sitting in a comfy movie-like chair at church, as they went over the morning announcements. Typically, I'm distracted during morning announcements as my friends are continuing to show up and I say hello and give hugs, but this Sunday, I was all ears, for some reason.

*Some reason, hmmm... *

As Jolene was standing on stage telling us all about the latest news with the church, she continued on talking about a mission's trip to Kolkata, India that was taking place in six months. She had said that the trip would be for two weeks in the most impoverished city in India, where the group would be working with blind orphans. Quickly, I was reminded of the dream I had the night before. During her talk, I felt like that literal light bulb was blinking over my head (again).

*Okay God, I'm hearing ya. *

God had shown me that dream of what I could only have described as a third world nation. I knew right away that this was my opportunity to go to India!

Jolene continued talking about the trip and as she did so, I was more and more enthusiastic. At the end, she said that if we felt it on our hearts to participate in the trip, to email her and she'd forward us more information.

Before she had even left the stage, I crafted her an email that said, "Jolene!! I'm coming to India! Sign me up!" And with that, I hit send.

With the trip, there were ten others signed up, each worried about how they were going to afford this expensive trip. Not me. Not once. I did what the church recommended with sending out letters and mentioning it to friends and family, which helped, but God really provided that money.

Financially, they had the trip broken down into smaller payments that could be paid off leading up to the trip. I would pay $300 each month from fundraising efforts and waitressing.

About two months into it, I got a rather large and unexpected check bonus check from waitressing what I took as a token from God. I took that check the very next day to the bank, cashed it, and wouldn't you know...it was the exact remaining portion that I had to pay for my trip. I went into that next meeting the following Tuesday with a wad of cash, looking like a p.i.m.p. and handed it straight over to my leader, knowing that I had zero worries or concern about India; it was just meant to be.

*Huh, okay God, I see you! The second time He provided the exact amount of money needed to fulfill His will. *

Leading up to India, I was elated. I had a whole list of things to get done before going, like researching culture norms and getting the twelve million vaccinations required at the travel clinic. I had traveled once out of the country before, but Asia would be a new travel experience for me.

The advice and stories I heard from others about India were almost like scare tactics. "You're going to be blown away by the poverty. India is the dirtiest and worst smelling area in the world. Rape! Never go alone anywhere because India is known as the number one sex trafficking place in the world!"

Everything people said would go in one ear and out the other, as nothing was going to set the tone for this trip. I didn't want to go into India with any preconceived notions or expectations; I just wanted to experience India out of the lens that God saw it. This is what I continuously prayed for leading up to the trip and during:

Lord God, I am grateful that I get to experience Kolkata. I don't know what I'm meant to see or hear, but I do know you have perfectly orchestrated this trip. I ask, dear Father, that you would reveal India to me in the exact way that you see it. Let me be open and willing to do whatever you lead me into. I trust you and I trust that your plan is greater. Thank you, Lord. In your son's name I pray. Amen.

*Some may have thought I was naïve; I was choosing to trust God. *

Fresh off the plane, the ten of us hopped on a cramped multi colored trolley, weaving in between traffic, as if no road rules had ever been created. With all windows open in the trolley, it was flashes of exuberant colors, men and women walking the sides of the streets with wicker baskets on their heads, and motorists swarming in and out of traffic. It was an absolute adventure. When the trolley man kicked us out and told us to walk the rest of the half mile distance to our hotel, I was in total amazement.

Just like I imagined and saw in my dream, roads that were rocky, cows and dogs roaming the streets aimlessly, little farmers markets on each corner, and smiling, loving faces in each direction. We all had to stop to try their famous chai tea as we approached the hotel we would be staying in for the next two weeks.

As we walked through the doors, we all instantly noticed that this wasn't your typical hotel, or at least an Americanized one. There was no padded carpet, no comfy bedding, no host stand, or even drinking water.

Noticing some major differences, my thoughts were interrupted by Azaan blaring over a loudspeaker that seemed to be right next to our window. We all stopped what we were doing in amazement. "What is that?" one would ask. "Why is that so loud?" another would question.

Once the buzz of the loudspeaker quieted, the leader of the group, Jolene, shared that it was a form of propaganda for the main religion in that region and no matter what people were doing, they were meant to stop and pray. By about the fourth time, we got the hang of it, but it didn't get any less jarring, blaring two times a day (one at the crack of dawn, another mid-day).

The following day, we all headed off to a local orphanage where we were told that these children just needed to be shown God's love. Jolene went on to say that some of the children would be blind and have lice and potential skin defects. Sure enough, that was exactly the case. No matter how different these children might have looked on the outside, they were no different from the kids who grew up near us; they just wanted to play, skip, hug, jump, and laugh. They showed no cares in the world.

I will never forget the most precious girl who wouldn't leave my side. Her name was Amoli. She was about six years old, with hair that didn't go past her ears. She had a huge smile that seemed to cover half of her face. Amoli was blind and most of her face looked as if hot candle wax had been poured on it. I had asked Olivia why so many children had faces that were scarred, like Amoli, and the story to follow broke my heart.

By now, most of us have seen *Slum Dog Millionaire*, and if you haven't, I encourage you to. From my short-lived experience in India, that movie is one hundred percent spot on to what I saw. Now with a few of us Americans surrounding her, Jolene went on to share, "A lot of these families cannot afford food, clothing, and basic items, so they have their young children go out and peddle for money. If the children aren't producing enough money, often times, the parents will pour hot wax or oil on their faces, skin, and bodies so that when they go out begging, people will feel bad for them and give them more money. If a child is born with a deformity from birth, the parents will do this to better increase their income. When this happens, the parents are taking the children out of school, so they aren't getting a proper education, but instead, are working to provide for their families."

Now more than ever I wanted to show these children unconditional love, just like their Father.
Playing on the playground with these students, we proceeded inside a Christian school, where these children were learning who

God was, singing, having fun, eating lunch, and playing during recess, just like kids their age should be.

On the second day, we went back to that school with a mission to help give the school a facelift with new paint. We were to give all four floors a fresh paint coat of lime green to liven the place up, hoping to boost morale within the school.

A few hours went by, we left the school feeling exhausted and ready to see what else India had to show us. Our leader, Jolene, got us back on the bus and explained that she was going to take us to meet a few people.

We stopped back off at our hotel for a quick shower & power nap, we headed to a Christian church nearby. There, we got to attend an Americanized-style service with a powerful message about God's never-ending love and ended with an intoxicating worship team. It was a fantastic service from a powerful pastor who loved the Lord and a choir who were eagerly rejoicing God.

Once the service was over, we headed to the basement where we ate a meal with the worship team, along with members of the community who were known for their evangelism.

All the Americans were told to separate and sit at different tables so that we could really get to know the others. I ended up joining a table with two beautiful Indian women who were a few years older than me and had been attending that church for over five years. They were both a part of the worship team and very active within their church community. Their passion and excitement when talking about finding the Lord and showing other Muslims who He is was inspiring and like a breath of fresh air.

*Why don't Americans have that same type of excitement, I wondered? *

On my right was a Southern belle from Georgia who could steal the whole room's attention when she walked in. Stella was absolutely gorgeous, with her wildly voluminous brown hair and dimpled cheeks. When she smiled, she took my breath away. There weren't moments when she wasn't was smiling, so I was breathless a Michael Phelps amount of time.

I drank in everything she said because I knew this was a woman of God; you could see it written all over her face. Stella was an evangelist who was living full time in India, preaching about the good news of God through the business she started.

One of the larger problems India is facing is gender equality, specifically the lack of opportunity for women to work and provide for their families. Stella created a business in which she employed local women to crochet, knit, and sew blankets. The amazing thing is that most women in that region had never received an income before; that was something only the men did, so by doing this, she was starting a ripple effect towards women's equality.

*How amazing is that? Yet again, I saw another opportunity for God to combine a personal passion AND working for His benefit, all at the same time! My mind is racing and intrigued! I know for sure that it wasn't a coincidence that I met her. *

One night, as we were enjoying an authentic Indian feast out at a local restaurant, Stella re-appeared toward the end of our meal with the blankets in tow. She showed off her prized possessions like they were rare diamonds and talked about each one with the unique story that followed suit.

"This gorgeous blanket was made by Pretti, a mother of five, who lives on the Eastern side of Kolkata…"

Once we all finished eating, we rushed toward the blankets, chose the ones we wanted, handed Stella our Rupees, and walked away knowing that this was contributing to a greater good.
This blanket meant so much more than your average blanket; this was going towards someone's future, someone's place within their household, and helping a nation towards female empowerment.
I bought a colorful orange patched blanket with brown and green stitching, and attached was a story of Ruthi, the woman who made it, and information about Stella's organization.

To this day, I still have that blanket and as I hold it, smelling some sort of curry blend, I get overwhelmed at the goodness of our God.

*How cool is it that God could chose someone, like Stella, with an open heart to show love and compassion, especially towards a population that doesn't often see that? I mean, come on! *

Days later, Jolene took us to a Christian hospital. Walking through this clean and sterile building, we were told that most luxuries of American hospitals, like a bed for each person, sterile instruments, animal-free spaces, and equipment were rarely found in the hospitals in Kolkata. They proudly said that they lean on donations given to them so they can have the highest satisfaction rating amongst the hospitals.

While taking the tour, one of the staff members told us that weeks before our visit, there had been a major fire at a nearby hospital. The four-story tall building caught fire and was quickly swallowed up. The staff ran out of the building, leaving behind the disabled elders on the top floor, the nursery, and their mothers on the second and third floor, along with all equipment. Within a matter of ten minutes, the whole building was engulfed in flames and it came crashing to the ground, with everything and everyone in it. Such a tragically devastating story.

He went on to share that two weeks before this fire happened, someone from America had donated a rather large and expensive fire hydrant system to go in their hospital to cover all their floors. After this massive fire hit the nearby hospital, officials went to check the other five hospitals to make sure they were up to code with having the proper fire procedures in place. Because none of the hospitals had fire protectants, the city closed them each down, until they could come up to code.

The only hospital left was the Christian based hospital that I was visiting, all because of that generous donation weeks prior. Praise Jesus! We all walked out of that hospital feeling blessed to have heard about another incredible miracle straight from the hands of God.

*Amen! That story still gives me shivers at the wonders of how God works! *

On this trip, we met many more evangelists who had given up their normal Americanized dream to be a part of the Indian culture; to be shining lights of Jesus.

By the last day, I was heartsick to leave. I was somber to leave these beautiful people who always had a smile on their face. I was saddened to leave somewhere where everywhere I turned, I saw color and imagination. More than anything, I was afraid that when I returned home, I wouldn't see that same fire for Jesus like I had in India.

****

An eighteen-hour flight later, I was back home in the States. It was time to return to my collegiate routine and work schedule. Now, I just needed to be patient to see what God had in store for me next.

Forever Changed Part-Two

Months away from being done with my final year of college, it all came to a crashing halt when I went to see my guidance counselor. Mrs. Helenoff proceeded to tell me that as a communication major, I was required to take two years of a language, which I had yet to do.

She spilled out my options bluntly and without any compassion added, "You'll have to stay an additional four semesters to finish the requirement, or you can complete it abroad. If you choose to study abroad, your choices are Mexico, Spain, or Venezuela."

Needing to make a snap decision, I knew my only option was to go abroad, as I sure as heck wasn't about to spend two more years taking this dreadful language.

At the time, there was an Ebola outbreak in Spain, so I took a hard pass being the one American to bring the next plague about.

I reasoned that I could go to Mexico any time I wanted, so I concluded that Venezuela was the choice for me, especially since it was the least expensive and most exotic sounding option.

I knew literally nothing about Venezuela; didn't know where it was on a map, the exchange rate, or what the people were like. I only cared about completing the language requirement as quickly as possible and moving on.

I hated Spanish. The Spanish I did take in high school and at my community college, I only passed based on others' help. Yes, I was that annoying student who totally clung on to the smart kids and copied their answers.

I truly believed that Spanish wasn't the language for me, and I just didn't have the capabilities to pick it up (thanks, enemy, for that positive affirmation). But I figured just like all my past experiences, I would fake it 'til I made it for a few months and come out of it graduated.

And with that, I had less than one month to prepare for my three-and-a-half-month full immersion program in Mérida Venezuela.

****

Before we knew it, the twelve of us Americans were at the Caracas airport, waiting to be picked up by our tour guide, Ramon. The airport was full of beautiful suave men and women of golden-brown skin, dark hair, and mouths that moved faster than pre-teens at a sleepover. Instantly, I felt intimidated by my lack of Spanish, in comparison to the rest of my American classmates. Feeling like I may have underestimated the importance of the language, we hopped onto a doorless bus to get the grand tour of the town we would be staying in for the whole summer.

Mérida was breathtaking, with mountain views from every angle, endless colors, and a hustling city life on the main streets. After spending the afternoon as a tourist in the city, I was excited to find out where I would be staying.

One by one, our bus dropped us off at the houses that we would be staying at for the duration of our trips, all in varying parts of the town. At my stop, another girl named Jacklyn hopped off with me, as we were going to be bunk mates. I was so excited, knowing that this poor girl was going to be carrying the Spanish load for the two of us.

Our house was clearly in the rich neighborhood with a brick three-story house and a gorgeous deck that wrapped around the entirety of the home, tucked away in a gated community. Jacklyn and I were shown our quarters, which was a large room with two twin size beds, separated by two dressers in the middle of the room. It was the perfect summer setup.

The next morning was our introduction to our new school. I was over the moon to see where I would be spending most of my time and to get familiar with the rest of the students at this English-Spanish immersion school.

I took a literal three-minute shower in frigid *Titanic* water, got dressed, and headed to the kitchen to find my host-mom, Zulema sitting there watching her Telenovelas. I swiftly looked over my shoulder several times to realize that Jacklyn wasn't by my side to help translate. Not wanting there to be dead space, I made brief conversation and said the basics, "gracias," "muy bien," and "si," because at this point, I was barely a Spanish beginner level one. Jacklyn had finished adding her notebooks to her JanSport backpack, as we grabbed a quick snack for later and hopped in Zulema's small pickup truck to head to school.

We pulled up to a slender green building tucked between a fence and a bodega. Printed on the front was the word *Venusa*. We excitedly strolled in to see someone sitting at the front desk. Jacklyn did all the talking to let him know we were new students, heading to our orientation. Walking down the hallway, we noticed a colorful bulletin board that proudly displayed all the American names, leading us into a larger main rec room with twelve chairs set up to face a projector. I settled into the hard plastic seat and studied the surroundings to see what this school was all about.

The principal of the school started her introduction, "Bienviendo a Mérida! Hola, me llamo Francis!" Noticing eyes darting across the room, she switched over to English and continued,

"Welcome to *Venusa*. My name is Francis. I am the principal, and I am here for anything you need. I will help with your family stay, questions about currency, complaints, or any concerns you may have. Please come and talk to me."

She proceeded to tell us we would have classes in the morning, a lunch break in the afternoon, more evening classes, then dinner at home. She then went into her scare tactic of telling us to watch out for Venezuelans, as they are very attracted to Americans, physically and monetarily.

"Do not have sex with a Venezuelan. The rate of STDs is very high, and you need to remain protected and focused on your schoolwork. Never do any drugs here or drink alcohol."

At this point, I was rolling my eyes, thinking, "These things don't pertain to me. Keep it moving, lady."

As she concluded her talk, she introduced Sonja as the next speaker. Sonja was the school's accountant. She told us that she was going to put our money into her safe at school so that we wouldn't risk our money being stolen, or lost. She went on to say that when we wanted to go on an excursion, we could go to her to collect our money. Sonja was right to the point, no fooling around, as if she'd had to repeat this talk verbatim every few months. Francis thanked her for her time and introduced us to the next busy bee at *Venusa*, Senora Noris.

Noris was the chef of the school. She was a beautiful woman who was very soft-spoken and only spoke in Speedy Gonzales Spanish. She quickly said that if we had any requests or allergies, to let her know. Otherwise, she looked forward to having us.
The last introduction was to a man named Juan. Instantly, I was attracted to him as he glided past me with an intoxicating cologne lingering in the air. He was handsome and tall, with dark features and a five o'clock shadow.

Juan let us know that he was there to help us with anything we needed, such as, converting currency, giving directions, or assisting us in our Spanish. Outside of those tasks, Juan would be collecting our food orders every day, bringing us lunch, and tallying up our expenses.

I didn't care what he was saying. All I could think to do was stare at that gorgeous mouth, wondering what his story was. As he walked away, I couldn't help but check him out as he grazed past me. I quickly snapped out of it when our tour guide entered back into the scene and told us that we were officially going to start school tomorrow but for the rest of the day, our guide, Ramon, was going to take us gringos to the mall.

The next day, I woke up early, ate a cheese and ham filled arepa prepared by my host mom, waited for Jacklyn, and we skipped to school, excited to find out what our classes were going to be like. We got into the main rec room and saw Venezuelans mingling with the Americans, already forming conversations, laughing, and exchanging numbers. I quickly formed a bond with a young girl named Adrianna who was a few years younger than me. Adrianna wore bright lipstick, tummy revealing tops, and always displayed a flirty smile, like she had a secret. She didn't mind that I could hardly speak Spanish and vice versa with her English. We laughed and enjoyed each other's company nevertheless.

I looked at the clock and noticed that I was a few minutes away from my class starting, so I headed down the hallway and up the three flights of stairs until I found my classroom.

Arriving with only a few moments to spare, I sat in the front row and waited for other students to join, anxious at what this class would be like. In walked a voluptuous woman with tight brown curls and a gap in her teeth that showed every time she smiled. She had a warmth about her, something that let you put your guard down right away.

"Hola Erica. Soy Ivette!"

She quickly explained in English that this was Spanish one, I was the only student, we were going to be speaking Spanish most of the time, and we were going to have fun. And that we did. I absolutely loved Ivette. She was funny, compassionate, and for some reason, had a soft spot for me.

Initially, when I went into her class, I was thinking that others would help me get through it, but because I was taking the class alone, I had no choice other than to learn the material and improve.

*What are the odds that I was by myself, out of all those other students? That is a weird coincidence! *

With each class only being three and a half weeks long, Spanish one breezed by in a blink of an eye. Each week, I would learn new information, then be quizzed on the content I previously learned.

Outside of learning through our Spanish book and chalkboard, Ivette would come up with fun games we could play together to better understand the lesson plan.

One Friday morning, Ivette had us go downstairs to the rec room where we found Juan sitting at a table, aimlessly scrolling on his Blackberry. Ivette called him over to see if he would play a game with us. Feeling flustered that we were sitting at the same table, we all three took turns playing a game Ivette had made up to help me better understand this week's grammar.

I'm sure to Juan it was silly and quite elementary, but to me it was helpful, and I enjoyed that we got to do it together. The time flew faster than the transition from spring to fall, and slowly but surely, Ivette was teaching me to become a better Spanish speaker. My confidence was building as I entered more conversations with the Venezuelan students.

Two nights a month, the school would host a mingling event for the immersion students and the locals. The first Nuevos Encuentros I went to, they brought in a spicy Latino who taught us how to dance Bachata. After, the Venezuelan students and Americans played Uno until the school kicked us out, around 11:30.

Somewhere between the dancing endorphins and the boost of confidence from my Latin classmates, I mustered up the courage to find Juan, who was hanging back by the kitchen on his phone. Trying to come off like the cute foreigner I was, I casually asked if he could show me where the laundromat was when he had time during the week. I explained that I've tried figuring it out multiple times but I had no luck. I said this while twirling my blonde pixie cut around my fingers. With his cool, calm, and collected manner, he agreed and asked me to meet him back at *Venusa* in the morning. The next morning couldn't have come soon enough. I grabbed my laundry bag and headed back to *Venusa,* only to spot this sexy six-foot-two, mocha skinned Juan, with a backwards baseball cap and sunglasses, leaning against his car. I about fell weak to my knees right there on the sidewalk.

I jumped into his navy Volkswagen and started forming innocent questions like what he studied in school and what he did outside of school. As I reflected on how proud I was that I got it all out in Spanish, I waited for his response. Juan opened his mouth and out came perfect English, answering my questions.

Interrupting him, I shouted, "What! You speak English? Why haven't we been speaking it this whole time?"

Juan let out a manly chuckle, "Yeah, I just got back from studying in Chicago for four months, where I learned English. I wasn't planning on coming back to Mérida, but something told me that my family needed me back home. Also, they don't want us to speak English with the Americans because that wouldn't help them improve their Spanish."

*Something told him to come back to Mérida, at the exact same time I was arriving...hmmmm...what do you have up your sleeve, God? *

I couldn't help but notice what a genuinely good man he was. Juan proceeded to explain to me that his mom, Noris, worked at the school, but he was just there helping, as he was in between civil engineer projects.

His plan was to stay in Venezuela for two more months, continue to trade his currency over with Americans, and head to Germany, where he had a job lined up. As I admired his drive and commitment, I was trying to gauge if there were any vibes that might have been between us. Forty minutes later and one puny load of darks, I thanked him for helping me out as he dropped me back off into the gated community.

I walked into my host home with my tail between my legs, knowing he just wasn't into me. He was far too good looking, mature and obviously already had a Selma Hayek waiting for him at home. And, let's face it, he couldn't possibly be attracted to a gringa with green eyes and blonde hair.

During lunch the next day, all of us Americans sat together and exchanged stories of what we'd experienced thus far. The guys of the group shared with us what they did the night before.

"Ah man, we went out to this club called *Racing* with Juan and it was so fun. We drank so much rum."

After that, all I heard was blah blah blah.

"Juan went?" I questioned, while hoping not to come off like I cared either way. I wouldn't have thought Juan would want to hang out with the Americans. Already having Juan's number from our laundry trip outing, I pulled my old school brick Nokia phone out of my backpack, ready to craft the perfect yet flirty message.

"Hi, it's Erica, the white girl. Do you want to come out with us tonight to *Bananas*?"

Within seconds, I got a text back. It read, "Hey! Yeah, that sounds like fun. What time?"

A few more texts went back and forth until the details were worked out. Since he had his own ride, he was going to pick up Jacklyn and me from our house around nine, then the rest of the group would meet us shortly after.

In the hours leading up to it, I was scheming about how I could win him over while simultaneously having him kick Selma to the curb.

Not yet crowded for a Saturday night, we found a table at *Bananas* right away. Knowing that there were going to be over twelve of us, I made a mad dash to sit next to Juan, thinking how I didn't want my schoolgirl crush to go unnoticed.

With the server coming around, all the girls ordered fruity daiquiris while the guys ordered Modelos. The group was lively, enjoying each other's company, but I didn't want to focus on that. I wanted to focus on Juan.

Juan went on talking about his experiences growing up and what he did in his spare time, and I would make sure to graze my hand on his shoulder while throwing my head back laughing over what he said. When that didn't seem to pick up much traction, I would move my foot under the table to tickle his ankle. Nothing worked. Every cliché trick I had seen in movies was a lie. Either he was really naïve or really not interested, I thought.

It was near bar close, so we all said adios and hopped into Juan's VW to head back home. He stopped in front of our host home and I quickly thanked him for driving us and leaped out, knowing that I should just move on.

*Selma, one. Erica, zero. *

* *

   It was a new week and I was about to start Spanish two. I was really excited about how everything had been going thus far and assumed the same would be true for my next class.
   Alongside my individual classes, the full immersion experience was really working. I was starting to really pick up the language and be able to have deeper conversations than just the "Hi, how are you? My name is." I was really looking forward to soaking in all I could from Ivette. During semester two, I spent the majority of my time with my American classmates and less with my head in the clouds, thinking about tall, dark, and handsomes, (at least for the time being).
   My weekends spent with the Americans were wild and adventurous. We saw the world's largest waterfall, Angel Falls; you know, the one from *Up*. We spent fifteen hours at the beach one Saturday, where I ended up getting third degree sunburn on my legs, (Ouch. I'll spare you the purple details.) We repelled down waterfalls, where I fractured my ankle (again, ouch.) While the experiences were one of a kind but also terribly painful, I felt that I might be missing the tradeoff of spending time immersed with Venezuelans.
   After sneaking away four weekends in a row, American style, I decided to switch it up and spend a full day with my new girlfriend, Adrianna. Adrianna didn't speak very much English, and at this point, I was still speaking at a Spanish two level, but either way, we had a blast together. We went to the market to buy souvenirs, slammed down beers and ham pizzas, went to a museum, and ended the night by going dancing at a club. That night, it was Adrianna, two other Venezuelan friends, an American classmate, and me. *Something* in me decided it would be worthwhile to give it another try with Juan.

*Hmm that's interesting... *

I shot him a text, asking if he'd like to join all of us girls out at the club (assuming his girlfriend wouldn't mind.) I was still trying to figure out what he thought about me, but I also wasn't interested in mind games, especially since I had my conversation with God about giving my dating life to Him. I told myself that night I would play it cool and give him his space.

The club, *Racing*, was packed; good looking Venezuelans shoulder to shoulder every way you looked, as they double fisted Coca Cola and Rum.

We made our way to a standing table and went in waves to go get our drinks. Once we all had our beverage of choice in hand, we stayed near the table, swaying to the Latin beats, laughing, and drinking the night away.

As Adrianna was about to leave me to go to the bathroom, I pivoted and made eye contact with Juan, making small talk about what was new with him. Sipping out of my straw and swaying to the music, Juan swiftly grabbed my hand and led me to the dance floor.

My heart was beating a million miles a second. "What is happening? Is he bored or something?" I pondered.

We made our way to the middle of the dance floor where he put his right hand on my lower waist, connected his left hand with mine, and pulled me close. The song was a fast tempo Prince Royce Bachata tune, meant to be danced to in very close proximity to your partner. The song was nearing the climax and as our bodies were shifting, our eyes locked. Juan added more pressure to my lower back until his face was inches from mine.

He leaned in and our lips touched. I felt butterflies in my stomach like this was all straight out of a movie. Everyone around us disappeared. The music had paused. I felt lightheaded because of the endorphins and possibly the rum. I couldn't believe that this was happening. I still felt like this goofy white girl who got invited to the prom by the sexy all-star quarterback. I couldn't believe he was kissing me.

*Erica, 1. Selma, 0. *

****

The next morning, I hustled into school with nerves up to my throat. I didn't see Juan all morning, which I was thankful for. Class was dismissed and as I was heading into the rec room for lunch, I spotted him out of the corner of my eye. I was desperately trying to avoid eye contact, as if that would shield him from seeing me.

He came up to our table and asked in his perfectly articulate Spanish what we all wanted to eat, completely avoiding what had happened the night before. I played along, ordering spaghetti and meatballs with a lemonade.

With no hinting towards the night before, I worked up the courage to shoot him a text once he was out of eye sight.

"I had fun last night. PS - you look cute today."

I hit send and my nerves went through the roof! I couldn't believe I just said that. What if he responded badly to that? What if he thought I was a freak? My thoughts got interrupted by a text.

"Me too. And you too, as always!"

My heart completely fluttered! Those words confirmed that he liked me too. I felt like I was in middle school all over again, but I didn't care. I was loving every silly crush moment.

Days went by and Juan still was playing it cool, not mentioning anything about the previous weekend. Sparks had flown between us with winks and giggles at school, but I didn't really know if he actually liked me.

As classes were over for the day, I headed to the rec room to gather up my notes and assignments when Juan strolled over to me.

My heart started beating as this tall glass of scotch came my way. In his deep, rugged voice, he said that he had an idea in mind and wanted to take me out on Saturday. "Our first date," I thought!

I said, "Of course," and waited excitedly for the weekend to arrive. Over the next few days, I planned meticulously with Jacklyn what I would wear and how I could keep my cool.

As we were finalizing my accessories of long dangling earrings versus the playful hair bow, Juan texted that he was outside the gate, waiting for me. I grabbed my sweater and bedazzled purse and bolted to the door.

It was around 6:00 when we set off on our first date. I asked him what the plan was, and he responded nonchalantly that I shouldn't worry about it. I sat back, enjoying the view (of him and Mérida) and started to tell him more about myself, what Minnesota was like, and what I was studying in college. Forty minutes passed and it looked as if we were leaving Mérida and entering into the country.

I asked where he was taking me, and with that sexy sly smirk of his, he responded, "Don't worry. We'll be there soon. Don't you trust me?"

With no hesitation in my mind, I said, "Yes, I do," and added jokingly, "But just know that next time you bring a girl outside of civilization like this, you may have to explain yourself."

As we proceeded talking about our bucket lists, Juan decelerated, pulling off to the side of the road to a 4' by 6' wooden wine cart. Juan bounced out of the car, handed some Bolivars to the elderly woman attending the cart, grabbed a bottle of pink wine, and came back to the car.

We continued driving for another ten minutes until the road wouldn't let us go any further. We were smack dab at the top of a mountain. Speechless, I watched as Juan got out of the car, grabbed the wine and plastic cups he had brought along, and motioned for me to follow him.

There was a brick paver that sat about five feet high, and Juan effortlessly sat on it, motioning for me to join. As I'm just slightly over five feet, I awkwardly lifted my body weight to sit next to him, hoping that I looked as graceful as it appeared in my head.

We were sitting facing the mountain and sighing at the beauty of the grayish mold entering seamlessly into the clouds. Juan poured us a glass of the rose colored, label-less, home-made wine and as I took my first sip, I savored the gorgeousness that was our date. Juan turned towards me and gave a soft kiss, then went back to staring at the mountain. We talked about all kinds of topics; education, our upbringings, our families, and our dreams.

Juan pivoted towards me and said, "You're really not like other girls. You go after what you want. You're crazy and I like that. I'm going to call you gringa loquita."

After feeling fairly confident that the feeling I had in my stomach was from him and not the delicious yet questionable wine, I turned to him in a serious manner and said, "I just want to let you know that there are two things that matter to me more than anything. Number one is God. And number two is that once I get back to Minnesota, I'm moving to New York. Nothing is going to interrupt that plan."

Juan looked at me with desire in his eyes and said, "I respect both of those."

Forty-five minutes later and ten degrees colder, we jumped back into his two door and back down the twisty road. As we entered back into town, we pulled up to a strip mall. Having zero expectations of what an international date would look like, I grabbed his hand and followed him up the stairs and into a fancy sushi restaurant. Already impressed by part A of the date, part B was going above and beyond my expectations.

Underneath plastic foliage and string lights, we found a table outdoors that seemed to have our names on it. A waiter came over, spat out fast instructions and placed menus in front of us. Juan caught the frazzled look on my face and ordered us something to drink, along with a shareable appetizer.

After what felt like a five-course meal, I was feeling so full of food and happiness over how our first date went. Once Juan paid the bill, like the true gentleman he was, we jumped back into his stick shift and headed back to my house to call it an evening.

As we sat outside the gates, I thanked Juan for the amazing time and for dinner. He put his hand on my chin and pulled me in for a kiss. I melted into him, like all fans did when watching Lady Gaga and Bradley Cooper's onscreen romance.

Minutes later, or hours (who really knows), I broke away and explained that I had to get to bed, being that I had a busy day ahead of me. With that, I half-walked, half-glided home, under the starry sky.

****

I was now entering Spanish three and was really loving my life in Venezuela. At this point, Juan and I had gone on several more dates. Each one was just as special as the last.

One date, he took me to a fancy hotel where we ate their ever-so-famous pizza with corn and ham slices, with a two-man band serenading us by our table. Then, there was another date where he took me to a rustic faraway lodge for cheesy ham and corn pizza (you can sense a pattern here.)

Another memorable night, but for a different reason, was on our sixth date. The burger joint's menu was so unique and I was mighty hungry. I ordered a burger with a large pineapple slice, cheese, and fried onion slices, mixed with barbeque sauce. As we were waiting for our burgers to be finished, we found a rustic picnic table outside and began preparing our endless napkins for the hefty task that was soon to come.

A few bites into the burger, my stomach began gurgling like *Free Willy* in a caught net. Within seconds, I knew. I was no stranger to these feelings, as I had been having intense stomach aches since I was twelve years old.

With urgency, I announced, "I'm sorry, but I need you to take me home right now."

Panicked and not sure if he did something wrong, Juan grabbed my green peacoat and together, we marched to his car.

Juan, looking at me with puppy eyes, inquired, "Are you okay? You're making me really nervous."

As I shifted around in my seat about a thousand times, I prayed.

Lord, we both know what's about to happen. I don't know why these happen or what lesson there is for me to learn but Lord God, please protect Juan from seeing this. Lord, let me escape before he sees me cry. Lord, be with me as I go through this unbearable pain in a foreign country. Lord God, please be with me. I need you. I need the Holy Spirit to help me through the pain that is coursing through my body. In your Holy name, Amen.

As we pulled up to my host house, Juan rushed out to open my door. I slowly made my way out of the car, with tears in my eyes, my arms wrapped tightly around my waist, hunched over, trying fiercely to make it inside in one piece.

Juan asked if he could come in to help me, but I insisted, "No, I'll be okay, really. Just go. We'll talk tomorrow."

Juan reluctantly agreed, "Okay, but text me as soon as you can so I know you're okay."

I pushed past the front gate and into the brick home, where I was greeted by a house guest who was also staying over the summer. Still in my unnatural stance, I hurried along the conversation by eagerly asking, "Donde esta Zulema?"

He pointed up the eight stairs and said it was the third room on the left. As fast as I could manage, I hurried up the staircase to the outside of her room where I knocked, weakly. Zulema came to the door in her thick pink robe and flip flops.

Just like a mom, she could sense something was wrong. Worried, she questioned, "Estas bien ella?" I forced out the words, "Zulema, I'm okay but I'm going to be sick for two hours. Please don't worry. I'll be okay. Can I just stay here with you?" As I really didn't want my roommate or my other classmates to know.

As soon as the words left my lips and Zulema started to creek open the door, my stomach gave out. That gave permission to unlock the beast that was inside me.

My appendix felt like it was going to burst. An invisible sword cut me through the middle. I laid helplessly on the floor, moving around in a million different positions until I could find one that felt comfortable in that millisecond. Tears of agony were strolling down my face as this demon in me was trying to come out of my stomach. Tears turned into screams and pain was now violent waves of catastrophe over my body.

I caught glimpses of Zulema, who looked like she was witnessing a murder right before her very eyes. At one point during the two hours, she gripped my shoulder and demanded that she take me to the hospital. Through moans, I let out that it wouldn't work, as it hadn't so many other times in the past. She pleaded to at least update the school with what was going on, but that only upset my stomach more as I roared, "No! Don't tell anyone."

As my two-hour time limit was about to be up and my stomach was having fewer violent attacks on itself, I laid in the fetal position on Zulema's bed until it died down. As I could feel the worst was behind me, I began inching my way off her king size bed, as I apologized for what she had just seen.

Still with a slight communication barrier, Zulema stood tall at four feet ten inches, in front of her door, demanding me to stay with her that night. Weaker than I had ever felt and not wanting to offend her, I closed my eyes right where I was and fell asleep, right alongside her and her husband, in their gigantic bed.

The next morning, I woke up not feeling like myself. The normal day-to-day activities like getting ready, eating, and walking to school, were exhausting. I felt like Casper's hung-over cousin, just floating along, not mentally a part of any conversation or activities. Walking into school was a blur. Emotionless, I shuffled past Juan.

He tapped me on the arm, exclaiming, "Are you okay? I was so worried about you last night. I never heard back from you. You really don't look good. Can I get you anything?"

I said nothing, as if this one-sided conversation never took place, and continued to my next class.

The moment Ivette saw me, she knew something was off. I had a test that Monday, and anything she may have said to advise me went in one ear and out the other. I blankly filled in the multiple-choice answers and once I was finished, like always, she sat next to me to correct the test. As she was going through, there were an awful lot of red markings, indicating I bombed the test.

Looking worried, Ivette pivoted in her seat and uttered, "Erica, are you okay? Because you really don't look well and this isn't a normal performance for you."

Knowing this was a completely new reaction for me after getting a bad stomach aches, I let it all out.

"Occasionally, I get very painful, crippling stomach aches that last two hours. I've been getting them for years but for some reason, the one last night was the strongest I've ever had before, like a tide completely took me under the water. It sucked all my energy, to where I now feel like a zombie. I can't eat. I can't smile. I can't even think. I don't know why these happen or why it's always two hours, but I know I'm not myself right now."

Ivette looked panicked, exclaiming, "I'm so sorry Erica. I'm going to postpone class and forget you ever took this test. Go downstairs to take a nap. We'll pick class up later, once you're feeling better."

*Wow, that was extremely generous of her! No other teacher has shown that type of sympathy towards me before. I knew she had a sweet spot for me, I just didn't know why... *

Feeling grateful about the test, I headed downstairs to find an empty hammock in the middle of the recreation room, closed my eyes, and dosed off.

Hours later, I heard commotion around me and realized that it was now lunch time, as twenty other students were chatting near me.

As I was getting re-oriented, Juan came over to me to say how worried he had been as he watched me sleep. He told me to pick anything I wanted to eat, and they were going to bring it out to me.

I sat at the table, guzzled water, and waited on my chicken marsala. All praise goes to Noris with her wonderful meals that can bring anyone back from the dead. Slowly, I felt like a Simms character whose life support was climbing up the ladder. I finished my side of vegetables and headed upstairs to find Ivette.

As soon as she saw me, she threw her arms around me, shouting, "You look like yourself again! Come, sit, let's see about taking this test together."

Spanish three was a success and throughout all my individualized courses, I received an A. As I was nearing the end of my study abroad experience, I was beginning to feel as if it wasn't my time to leave just yet.

*What an interesting and random thought that came out of nowhere... *

It dawned on me that I would still have to return home to take Spanish four at a collegiate level and still push back my graduation, which was a huge bummer. My brain went into fast thinking mode.

Waiting for Juan to pick me up for yet another one of our dates, I had a feeling this date could be bittersweet as I was nearly at the end of my trip. He gave me a quick kiss as a hello, and we set off to a rose garden.

The day was a cool eighty-five degrees with a touch of sadness in the air. We held hands like young couples do, talking about what Germany would be like in the fall and how my last semester at the University would be. We aimlessly walked around the different plants and roses, drifting away, until we stumbled upon the perfect bench.

Juan turned to me, very seriously, and inquired, "You're leaving soon. What are we going to do?"

Completely thrown off, I stuttered, "Well, um, I don't know. I mean, I really like you, but you're leaving for Germany and I'm heading home then to New York."

Not content with my answer, Juan pressed on, "Well, we could try dating long distance."

Feeling giddy and flattered that this crazy white girl meant so much to him, I pushed on with the realities, "I only have a week and a half left, then I'm leaving. I'm going to have to go back to school for another semester, unless they let me take it here but..."

As I was thinking through the next part of this sentence, Juan jumped in, "Well, why don't you just take it here?"

Thinking about what he just said, I leapt off the bench and said, "That's a great idea! I don't see why they wouldn't let me! I'll ask when I get back to school."

And with that, we felt like we had just given ourselves and our summer romance a second chance.

The next day at school, I marched to the head principal's office with my head held high, to state my claim. "Hi, I'm Erica and I have taken Spanish one through three with you. I would love to stay another three and a half weeks to finish Spanish four, versus going back to my university to take it. Am I able to do that?"

She sheepishly looked at me and replied, "It is fine by me, if it is fine by your university."

Half of the equation was solved, I thought! Now I just needed to get my university on board. I called my mom and dad to plead my case, knowing how much it made sense, because of the cost difference and how much more I would excel in Venezuela versus in a classroom setting at the University. With all the facts presented, they agreed that it sounded like the right move.

With dial up like-internet, I rang the university and stated my claim. They bounced me around to many different people within the learning abroad office, all with official sounding answers until I finally got in touch with the program director. Now I felt like I was getting somewhere.

I re-stated my case and exclaimed that I would gladly pay to stay for another accelerated semester in Venezuela versus coming home to take the one course on campus.

The man on the other end of the line huffed hesitantly and said, "You know, we've never done this before. But I suppose if you send me these new forms signed, get your dean to sign off on it, and send your payment, you can stay."

I rushed to get everything submitted until finally, I received an email from the University telling me that I was approved to complete Spanish four in Venezuela, with days to spare!

*I was the only student to ever do that...interesting, and only days before, I was able to stay. Coincidence? *

I ran downstairs to shout the good news to Juan, who unbeknownst to my parents or dean was a small part of why I wanted to stay. Juan took me out that night to celebrate with beer and pizza, as we basked in our win.

A few nights later, we were getting ready to go out for a goodbye party for the other eleven Americans who were heading home. We got dolled up that night and went out to a new bar called *Elephante. Elephante* was an intimate, two floored bar that had a real Havana vibe.

Amongst the Americans were new Venezuelan friends. We ordered beers and tequila shots, and laughed the night away with the sweet memories we cultivated over the last three months. As the night was coming to an end, we all sat around outdoor tables, sharing our memories of the summer we spent together.

One girl, in her drunken accent let out, "Juan, who is that girl?" pointing directly at me. Juan casually let out, "Erica? Oh, that's my girlfriend."

My eyes lit up brighter than the Northern Lights. I knew Juan liked me, but this was the first time I had heard him put labels on us. This was the first time that I got a real sense of clarity about his feelings for me. Smiling from ear to ear, I left that night knowing I meant so much more to Juan than he let on.

* *

Spanish four was about to begin. I had now switched over to working with Rosa, Ivette's sister, and was loving it just as much as I had with Ivette. The content was getting meatier, but my understanding had also grown immensely. By the time I was in her class, I was almost bilingual, which is light years from where I thought I would be.

Wanting to finish on a strong note, I knew I had to do well on the final project, that was just less than two weeks away. The final project was a spoken presentation, with a listening and writing test. I studied during all my free time and even managed to scale back being with Juan to ensure a good grade.

The final three weeks passed by in a blink of an eye, and the final day was finally upon me to give my presentation. I was so nervous, knowing that everything was riding on how well I did. If I failed, having stayed the extra semester wouldn't have paid off. But if I did pass, Venezuela would have been a beautiful surprise and fun college experience that I'd never regret.

I was in the rec room finishing up my Juan-made brownie for good luck when I marched back upstairs to my class to knock the socks off Rosa.

I was told to pick a topic that I was passionate about for the speaking section of the presentation, so, I chose to speak about Tanya and the wedding dress. Two hours later, I walked out of that class with a bit of a swag and a final grade of an A.

Side note: Thinking back to when I first arrived over four months ago, I was planning on coasting off other people's Spanish and believing the enemy's lie that I wasn't smart enough to learn the language. Now, I had no one to lean on but my own knowledge and drive. I couldn't have been prouder of myself.

*Is that what Proverbs 3:5 means? Was I leaning on my own understanding and not trusting God? YUP, sure was. *

I had one final weekend left before I headed home, and I spent every single minute wrapped in Juan's arms. We were like Allie and Noah from *The Notebook*, minus all the arguing. Both not knowing if this was just going to be a summer romance, we had planned to try to date long distance until one of us said otherwise.

I woke up on Sunday morning with lots of mixed feelings, knowing it was my last day in Venezuela. I finished packing my bag, headed to the kitchen to finish my cheese filled arepa, gave Zulema a tight squeeze, said goodbye to the rest of my host family. I ran outside to soak in the final sun-filled moments before Juan arrived. Short lived, Juan pulled up through the gate and jumped out of this Volkswagen to help me load my oversized purple luggage.

We headed off to the airport together in what seemed to be the world's quietest car ride. Forty minutes later, we pulled into the airport parking spot, parked the car, and sat in silence.

Juan turned towards me and said, "Here, I have something for you."

He pulled out a shiny silver box with a purple ribbon on it. Like any girl receiving a present, I shrieked. I opened the box slowly, knowing that whatever was in this box represented how he felt about me. I pulled out a gorgeous set of pearl earrings, on top of a square silver diamond mold. "Oh, I love them!" I exclaimed as I threw my arms around his neck.

He got out of the car, grabbed my bags from the trunk, and we headed towards the airport entrance. Still holding hands, we waited in line for my plane ticket and yet another line to drop off my luggage. When he wasn't allowed any further, we embraced each other with warm hugs, kisses, and a quick "this isn't it" pep talk.

We were going to try dating long distance, knowing that if it didn't work out, at least we tried.

I found a seat in the miniature sized airport, waiting for my plane to board. Twenty minutes later, I was USA bound.

* *

Now that I had completed my final requirements to graduate, I had to figure out all of the other components surrounding the graduation; the ceremony, inviting friends and family, picking up my diploma, and getting my job back now that I was home.

As I was busy putting these missing links together, I rushed home to fill Juan in on the details. He was so much more handsome than I remembered. His five o'clock shadow had turned into six and he had let his hair grow longer than I had seen it before. On every call, I made sure to remind him that if he wanted to back out, he could at any time. And yet, he didn't.

After a few months passed by, Juan confessed on our morning call, "Your birthday's coming up and I want to be there for it!"

My face said it all, "I would love that!" I waited patiently as my birthday month approached, knowing it was going to be the best birthday yet.

****

You may be wondering what happened with those crazy stomach aches that I got. Well, after many trips to the doctor, hospital visits, unnecessary procedures, and food trackers over the course of fifteen years, I still had no answers.

Because of this, it built quite a mistrust with doctors and the medical industry. Having a medicine cabinet stocked with Vicodin and Percocet at the age of twelve wasn't quite the Band-Aid solution I was hoping for.

Fed up with the daily discomfort, I tried following my mom's dietary restrictions and gave up gluten. Ever since the summer of 2016, I have been gluten and stomachache free!

*Praise Jesus! *

After feeling worlds better after cutting out gluten, I decided to take it a step further for my health. I became vegan and all around homeopathic in 2018. Mentally and physically, I have never felt better. It's a beautiful testament to God and a beautiful reminder every day that my body, just like yours, is truly a temple worth protecting.

Unwavering

Let's back up the story for a second though. Before I went to Venezuela, I put my job on hold at a bridal store in the cities. When I got back home, I dialed their phone number and asked to speak to the manager.

"Hi Annette! This is Erica." Silence. "I worked for you before I went to study abroad for a few months..." Silence. "Well, I'm back and was seeing if my job was still available..."

Annette seemed to be shifting in her seat. "Well, we were prepared to offer you back your job with you coming back after three months, but unfortunately, now it has been closer to five so we had to give your job away."

Annoyed, I said my goodbyes and hung up the phone, needing to think fast about my next move. I told myself that I would pray on it overnight.

The next morning, I received a phone call from an unexpected caller.

"Hi Erica! This is Jordan. We're in sort of a pickle and would love it if you came back to work with us. We're looking to fill our manager position, as I'll be leaving the shop next month. Will you stop in so we can further chat about it?"

Feeling a rush of excitement at how quickly God had answered my prayer, I got dressed, threw a bow in my hair, and headed to the same bridal salon that I had met Amber at many months before.

I listened intently to what she was offering with the manager role. She continued talking about her upcoming move to Barcelona, and how while there, she was going to do the bridal buy for the store. As soon as I heard that, all her other words turned into a blur.

Side note: it had always been a bucket list item for me to go to bridal fashion week. The three years that I had worked at their salon, I had pleaded every single year for them to let me go, and each time the answer was a resounding no.

Back in: After hearing everything she had to say and the predicament she was in, I shared with her that I had just returned home from a summer abroad trip, recently graduated college, and was only here as a pit stop before heading to New York.

I explained that I couldn't accept the manager position because I would be leaving in six months, but I would happily work all the hours she needed in exchange for letting me go to bridal fashion week in Spain and assist doing the buy. Jordan could see my wager and how hungry I was.

She paused, knowing how desperate the store was and let out, "If you buy your own ticket, then you can come." And just like that, I was packing my bags, ready to jet off economy style to my next abroad destination.

****

All festivities surrounding bridal fashion week made up two days on my itinerary, but I knew I wanted to sightsee as much of Barcelona as I could. I headed to the airport, made my connecting flight, and was off to Barcelona.

While I could hardly contain my excitement, I looked over to the beautiful blonde next to me to see if her excitement would match mine. Sure enough, it did. I kid you not, she had a show-me-your-teeth smile the entire thirteen hours we flew.

This girl instantly caught my attention and I knew I needed to make an introduction.

I started off by asking why she was heading to Barcelona, only to find out that she was going to spend time with her long-distance boyfriend who she had been dating for over four years. Amazed by their commitment, I inquired how long they had been separated, what they planned on doing during their trip, and any other TMI detail for a stranger on a plane. Paola gladly answered my questions with the same level of excitement and teeth showing. She turned it over to me, inquiring what I was doing in Barcelona.

I tried to hold my excitement back, but instead blew my cover by shouting, "I'm here for work. I'm attending bridal fashion week." Amazed, she flung questions back at me like rapid spit fire. I instantly clicked with her and didn't want the plane ride to end because of how much I enjoyed our time together.

We talked about the difficulties of dating long distance and the similarities that we were both midwestern gals dating fine looking Latinos. Once the plane landed, she gave me her number and told me to text her at some point during my trip so we could get together. And with that, she pointed me in the direction of the correct bus I needed to take, and she disappeared into the crowd. I headed towards the mega bus she pointed me to, elated that my journey was about to begin.

On the last bus stop, I got off at Plaza de Cataluna, having only a map with printed hostels that were nearby. I headed west in my black pointed Macy's heels and two wheeled luggage to find where I'd be staying for the next eight days.

I wandered around aimlessly, taking in the beautiful Spanish architecture, the bustling of quick walkers, and the blue skies. After walking for thirty minutes and knowing my blisters were fresh, I stopped at a bench to get a better grip of where I was heading.

I asked the elderly woman who strolled slowly near the bench where La Rumbla was, which to my surprise was two blocks from where I was sitting. I headed two blocks over and as I was walking, stumbled across one of the hostels on my list. I felt so encouraged that I was capable of doing all of this without fear of being intimidated or lost.

*Thank you, Jesus! I couldn't do it without you! *

I walked into the hostel, told the young gentleman that I needed one bed, nodding, "Yes, a shared room is fine," and proceeded to leave my items behind. I put my items in a school-style locker, switched out my shoes for some sneakers, and went back out into the open air. Feeling independent and free, I took a deep breath and headed back towards the square where I had seen hop on, hop off buses.

I waited in line, grabbed my seat on the upper deck, and had my finger ready on the trigger for tourist pictures. Now, I'm not one to overly enjoy the touristy things like museums, famous buildings, and other artifacts, but I knew I had to make a stop at the world-famous Barcelona soccer stadium.

As Juan is their biggest fan, (Go Messi) I wanted to take pictures and even get him an authentic jersey from their stadium gift shop. After waiting in what felt like the longest line at Six Flags to get a jersey, I jumped back onto the hop on, hop off bus and departed back to the town square.

Tired and jet lagged, I went back to my hostel, checked into my twelve-bunk room, and found a lower bunk that just screamed "Erica."

Two hours later, I was abruptly awoken by candy wrapper sounds crinkling near my head. Curious, I bounced out of bed and looked to see where the noise was coming from. A curly headed hipster in her Bob Marley shirt and ripped not-so-ironically jeans looked down at me with a smile, "Sup?"

"Hey, I'm Erica. I'm your lower bunk mate. How's it going?"

After twenty minutes of chatting, I found out that Nordine had taken time off from her California life to travel and find herself, which, selfishly, I coveted. Knowing she was off to the next place on her list after Barca, I gave her my number and told her that if she wanted someone to grab dinner with to let me know. I walked away excited that I had already made two friends and hoped that I would run into either of them again on my trip.

The first two days, I wandered around from the east to the west, stopping in pastry shops, taking shots of cappuccino, and attempting to buy authentic souvenirs.

On the third day, I looked down at my Android and noticed I had a text message from Paola. Overjoyed that she reached out to me, we set plans to meet at the town square in one hour. I raced home, changed my clothes, and headed back to the square, not knowing what was in store.

We saw each other from across the way, went in for a big hug like we had been long lost friends, and from there, I followed her lead as she was an expert of Barcelona.

Craving a snack, we stopped into a local pub and ordered a plate of tapas and red sangria. Multiple sangrias later, we headed to the local university where we met up with Antonio, Paola's boyfriend.

Watching their innocent love as their fingers intertwined, whilst staring into each other's eyes, really made me miss Juan. I said a quick prayer, hoping that the next time I saw him we would be just like that.

Antonio showed us around his university and explained the history with each building until it became too dark to see what he was pointing at. I told them that I was going to head back to my hostel but said that I hoped we could do this again.

The next day when I woke up, I headed down to the common lunchroom where a bunch of other twenty-somethings were eating their fruit loops and toast while planning their day out. Not knowing exactly what I was going to do, I finished my yogurt and headed outside to see what the day would bring. I walked around some shops, exploring and getting lost until around lunch time when I headed back to my hostel to grab a sweater.

Footsteps from my hostel, I passed my bunkmate, Nordine. "Hey! Erica, right?" "Yeah, hey! How's it going?"

Nordine was with a guy named Trevor who also bunked in our room. Trevor and Nordine's styles fit well as they both looked like they had no idea what time it was or where their next haircut was coming from. I proceeded to ask what they were up to and they said, "We're headed to the beach. Wanna come?"

I hadn't yet been to the beach and was excited that I would get to experience it while in Barcelona, so I excitedly agreed. The three of us walked for what seemed like a mile and a half to get to the beach and when we got there, it was like seeing a whole new part of the country.

Trevor threw out a casual, "Let's go buy some lunch and beers and eat by the water."

I shyly let out, "Isn't it illegal to drink beer in public?"

They looked at each other with a kind of smirk like they had just realized my naivety. "Anywhere you have a beer is public."

I followed them inside a market where we grabbed the essentials; a loaf of bread, baloney, cheese, mustard, and a pack of beer.

With my new reputation of being a rebel, we sat down and made our very-dry mustard baloney sandwiches, shared our life experiences, while taking back a cold beer. Life felt so sweet. I couldn't believe how nice every single person I had met had been and how quickly we all formed friendships.

*In a time that I could have felt lonely, God provided me three new friends to enjoy my impromptu work trip with. Coincidence? *

Even though it was painfully evident to Nordine and Trevor that I was the innocent, untainted one of the group, they laughed at my lack of experiences and enjoyed my company nevertheless.

As the sun was beginning to set, we started our trek back to our hostel. Arriving back at my bunk, I quickly grabbed my charger and raced to the rooftop to video call Juan. I excitedly told him all about my trip thus far and the awesome people I had met. I could see the time difference caught him at a bad time so with that, I blew him a kiss and said goodnight.

The next morning, I woke up to a text message from Paola. She said she had the whole day free because Antonio would be in classes and asked if I wanted to hang out. Happily, I jumped in the freezing and communal showers, put on one of my cutest outfits and funky Pronovias style hats, and headed out to meet her in the town square. We linked arms and headed off to find the nearest paella and sangria for an early lunch.

* *

My final two days surrounding bridal fashion week had finally arrived. Checking into the all-expense paid five-star hotel, we stopped in the lobby around three in the afternoon for a socializing hour. Kleinfelds' Mara, Dorothy, and Sara were all mingling, along with Pronovias executives, as they sipped their expensive bubbly out of glass flutes. Jordan and I joined in, introducing ourselves to shop owners and wholesalers alike. Two mimosas later, we headed up to our room to unpack and take a baby cat nap before having to get ready for the runway show.

The evening of the runway show was a glamorous display of black-tie gowns and fashionistas (Chiara Ferragni and Whitney Port, to name drop a few), along with the total red-carpet experience. Photo ops prior to taking our seats in the sixth row gave us the feeling of royal treatment. After taking close to thirty selfies, the lights began to dim, indicating the show was about to start.

Gown after gown came gliding down the starry night walkway until the firework display finale, showing off a gorgeous ivory lace bridal gown with a four-foot detachable train.

*Thank you, God, for caring about my dreams and making them a reality. *

The final day with Pronovias consisted of a full day event, selecting gowns for our store back in Minnesota. The task was to walk through a beautiful white warehouse, aka the Italian Pavilion, and choose fourteen gowns that we wanted to carry in our store for the following year. Man. Talk about hard choices. There were nearly one hundred and thirty dresses of beautifully styled mannequins that were styled from head to toe to choose from. Each attendee was allowed to pause mid-day from the excruciating decision process to have a catered buffet style lunch.

I chose to sit at a table that I had heard were major influencers within Pronovias. On my right sat Victoria, the director of Pronovias, as well as three wholesale representatives, working all throughout the United States. I went to Spain, very strategic with a plan to secure a job in New York. After learning more about Victoria, I let no time pass before asserting that I had full intentions of meeting her, in hopes that she would allow me to work at their flagship store off fifth Avenue in New York.

Once our lunch was over, I reconnected with Jordan, went back to the difficult chore of narrowing down our options, and went back to the hotel for a power nap. Later that evening, there was going to be a party as a thank you for all the collaborators and partners of Pronovias at the Museu Nacional d'Art de Catalunya.

After taking many, many gorgeous Instagram-able worthy pictures in front of the fountain, we made our way inside. In our stunning Pronovias gowns, we danced our way through the crowd of influencers, runway models, leaders within Pronovias, and other shop owners until we reached our designated table.

As I gazed into this stunning, brick building with the perfect low light ambience, waiters began bringing rounds of red and white wine over, making sure our glasses were never empty.

After a delicious three course meal of epically small proportions, Jordan and I went our separate ways to mingle with the contacts we knew.

I spotted Victoria from a few tables over and headed her way. Making small talk, I asked how her daughter's school trip went, reminding her that I had paid attention from our previous conversation and nodding intently when she talked.

I could tell she wanted to ditch me like a bad first date and move onto more fiesta related matters, so I quickly pulled out my card and smiled, "I'm going to go find Jordan and make her dance with me, but in the meantime, here is my contact information. Once I get back home, I'd love to shoot you an email and work out the details of becoming your newest bridal consultant in August in New York." And with that, I skipped off, knowing that I did all I could.

My trip was coming to an end and I was looking forward to relaying all the fun experiences I had in Spain to my friends and family. I dialed Juan's number on WhatsApp, ready to tell him all about my time spent with Pronovias.

God is Calling

The week had finally arrived when Juan was coming. At this point, I was like the overly excited kid holding the piñata stick at a birthday party, just waiting to bust it open and retrieve my delicious chocolate prize.

It was a gorgeous Tuesday afternoon when Juan's flight arrived to Minnesota. I parked the car and was walking toward baggage claim, where we had planned on meeting.

As I was strolling through the airport, I had rushing thoughts of, "What if he doesn't like me as much as he thought he did? What if the chemistry isn't there anymore? What if he realizes this was a mistake?"

*Enemy STAND DOWN! *

I sat on the cold black bench, hoping that would calm my nerves as I watched the clock with laser beam focus. Realizing very quickly that that didn't help, I stood up to walk over to the black and white arriving and departing screen. Seeing that Juan was now in Minnesota, I grabbed my clever, yet flirty sign, "I'm here for Juan" and said a quick prayer.

Dear Father, Juan and I are about to be reunited and I am so excited. I am so grateful that our paths crossed. I don't know what's going to happen while he's here, but God, I just ask that you remind me of the prayer I said to you all those months back. I trust in you, Lord God, that you know who is right for me. I don't have to force it or worry; You've got this! Thank you for flying Juan over here safely. I pray over Juan and his trip here in the United States. I love you with my whole heart and soul. Thank you, Lord, for loving me the way that you do. In Jesus' name, Amen.

Every second felt like hours and every sweat bead on my palm began to itch. Finally, I saw a rush of people come down the escalators, and I assumed Juan was going to be a part of the mob.

Like a kid scouting out his Easter egg basket, I laid my eyes on him, finally. Cleanly shaven, hair slicked back with an olive-green sweater that made his eyes pop, he forced his way through the crowd, elbowing his way to get to me.

I waited until he was fully off the escalators before rushing into his arms. We met in the middle of the baggage claim ten, gave each other the warmest embrace we had ever given, let our lips stay as one until they felt the need to part, and stayed in the moment completely alone.

When we finally separated, I couldn't believe it was him. I couldn't believe that hunk from *Venusa* was my boyfriend and was visiting me after we had been dating long distance for three months. We grabbed Juan's bag from carousel three and stayed morphed as one as we searched for my VW Passat.

Excited to show him around Minnesota for the first time, I figured he would be hungry, so I took him to the best pizza shop in the cities, knowing pizza was his favorite. We scarfed down a large pizze, drove around the Twin Cities to see the major attractions, and headed back to my two-bedroom apartment, where Laura and I both lived.

When we got inside and all settled, we sat down to have "the talk." Juan was in the United States as a tourist on a six-month visa, so it was decided that while he stayed, he'd have to find somewhere else to live or worst-case scenario, slum on my couch.

We had decided that we were going to take it one day at a time. I continued to tell Juan that if at any point he wanted to terminate our relationship and head home, that I would respect his decision. And I truly felt at peace with those words.

At this point, I had introduced Juan to Olivia, along with my other best girlfriends, but was now mentally preparing for heading over to my parents' house the next night to introduce Juan for the first time.

We pulled up to my parents' house, hand in hand, ready to take the questions and interrogations. Sitting in front of a lovely all-American meal with three hefty portions of a meat, carb, and vegetable, my parents moved forward asking about his family, what he studied in college, what his plans were with his career, and all-in-all trying to get a better sense about his intentions. After the longest three-hour dinner of our lives, we left feeling mentally beat up from all the questioning but at last, happy to be together.

After a few weeks had passed in our pure infatuation bubble, Juan declared that he wanted to stay longer than just a few months. He was really liking the United States and wanted to contribute to this life that we were on the brink of forming. Though Juan couldn't work due to his visa limitations, he wanted to make sure that when I got home from a long day of work as a server that he would have dinner made and a clean house to come home to. We were both feeling like a well-oiled machine that was meshing very well together.

A month into his stay, we made a stop at a gorgeous park, which surrounds a scenic pond where you can go paddle boating, golfing, and take scenic pictures.

We were walking hand in hand, enjoying the beautiful fall weather with the snow starting to melt over the pond and the fall-colored leaves that were transitioning to white. We found the perfect bench underneath a willow tree, where I grabbed the ham, tomato, and cheese sandwiches I had made from my bag for an impromptu lunch.

In this picturesque moment, we were nestled together, enjoying people watching and our sandwiches, when Juan pivoted his body towards me and said, "Erica, I have really enjoyed our time together. I love you."

The air rushed out of my lungs. I had no words. I was completely overwhelmed at how much this human meant to me and in such a short period of time. This relationship with him was like none other I had ever experienced. We had zero expectations of each other. We always gave each other the opportunity to terminate the relationship at any time, making sure we weren't compromising our dreams and now, he had confessed his love for me.

We finished our sandwiches, made our way through the rest of the path, and headed home. Meanwhile, I was still completely out of words. (Sorry Juan!)

The next day we set out to go tour Minneapolis some more. As we were packing another lunch in the kitchen together, I turned to Juan, grabbed his hand, looked deep in his big brown eyes, and professed, "I love you too, Juan."

As if we weren't inseparable enough, this made us an icky lovesick couple. Anyone who was around us thought we were "too much" or "over the top," but we didn't care. We were head over heels. And the amazing thing was, I wasn't thinking about next steps. That part of relationships where you constantly wonder about timelines and where things are going never happened. Just like every other thing in our relationship, we took it day by day.

*If this is what happens when you give it over to God, sign me up for giving over EVERY area in my life! *

I said goodbye to Juan in the afternoon as I headed to my waitressing job for my six-hour dinner shift. When I got home, I was physically exhausted from running back and forth, waiting on needy guests, and was starved for some food of my own.

I opened the door and saw candles lit and a freshly prepared dinner on the table. Over the moon that dinner was already prepared for me, I sat down with a goofy smile on my face. It wasn't unlike Juan to light candles to make the mood a bit more romantic, but this particular night, it sure was a nice touch.

As I hooved cheesy mashed potatoes into my mouth, Juan was babbling on about how he only had a few months left on his visa before it expired. It was like he was talking out loud, trying to work out how he could extend his time in the U.S. Meanwhile, I was just wanting to interrupt to find out what was in those dang potatoes.

Trying to help a man out though, I added that he ultimately had three paths: He could enroll into a university for a Master's program, but that would mean he/we'd have to stay in Minnesota for at least another two years. He could re-apply to stay as a tourist for another six months, but chances were low he'd get accepted. Or, he could try to start his own construction business in the United States under an entrepreneur visa. Half concentrating on what he was saying and half moving onto my green beans, Juan was still working through everything I said until suddenly, silence filled the air.

Juan shifted in his chair, stared intently into my eyes, grabbed my hand, and said, "Well, I know what I want to do. I want to spend the rest of my life with you. Erica, will you marry me?"

Trying to comprehend what just happened, I threw down my napkin and shouted, "Yes!"

No ring. No photographer. No family waiting to jump out. Simply a man who decided on the spot what he wanted for the rest of his life.

Now that we were officially engaged, we had to think logically about how we could get married before his visa expired. Through a lot of discussions, we decided to hold off on any plans until we told my parents the news, which wouldn't be until after New Year's (two months later)!

For those of you that are thinking I was crazy, I'll explain my logic. My parents had only met Juan two or three times before he proposed and were already a bit on the fence about our whirlwind romance. Out of respect for them, I pretended to not be engaged until after Christmas, ensuring proper permissions from my stepdad.

Into the New Year and with Gary's blessing, we had decided that our wedding was going to be in March, just two months away from when we "announced" our engagement. Luckily for me and all my years in bridal, I knew the best shortcuts and cost-effective ways to have the dream wedding with the most amazing husband-to-be.

Just like our love, our wedding plans were a whirlwind. One day, we were talking about getting married at the courthouse. The following day, we were set on getting married at the park where Juan first confessed his love to me. Our plans were all over the place week to week. The only things I was set on were that I didn't want bridesmaids or many attendees, I wanted a Christian service, and I wanted us to go through marriage counseling before entering into such a big commitment.

****

Wednesdays became a very trying day for us each week. When Wednesdays came around, we knew that as a couple we were going to face some difficult topics.

"How many babies do you want? Do you want to raise them believing in fictional characters? Whose role is it going to be to do house chores?"

We would leave most weeks ready to pull each other's hair out, over these large topics that had never even come up during our dating period.

A few weeks into the program, my pastor had asked about a stress point in our relationship and we voiced simultaneously, "The wedding!"

Out poured all the unmade, uncommitted decisions that were weighing our shoulders down until the pastor queried, "Well, have you considered getting married here?"

Like someone had just done the ice bucket challenge over my head, I let out, "I didn't even think about that! I would love to."

After panning out some details, it was confirmed that a month later, on Wednesday the 23rd, when the church didn't have any conflicting events, we would become the Barreto's.

Now that we had a location set, it was much easier for me to wrap my head around what I should be wearing the day of.

Olivia, my mom, and I went from bridal shop to bridal shop, trying to find the perfect off the rack gown that felt right. Exhausted from a long day of kissing frogs, I declared that I only had the energy to go to one last shop before throwing in the towel. We backtracked and went to the bridal shop that only months earlier wouldn't rehire me after my return from Venezuela.

I casually peeked at their large off the rack selection and grabbed a cute t-length lace number. I liked what I saw in my private fitting room, but the real test was, would the girls?

I came out of the private room wearing brown ankle boots and an ivory strapless A-line lace gown, giving off a real country vibe. Both had their mouths wide open and exclaimed that it was (finally) the right one. And thank goodness because we were only twelve days away from the wedding!

Our wedding day had finally arrived. It was a gorgeous winter, errr, blizzard, day in March. As my family alerted me of the drama, all I could think was, "Man, this is going to make for some gorgeous pictures!"

*Thank you, Lord for allowing me to see the positivity in situations and hearing your thoughts above others! *

My team of girls all headed to the hair salon at ten in the morning to begin the beautifying process.

A few mimosas deep and feeling quite relaxed, I was getting text alert and phone calls from wedding guests wondering if the wedding was still proceeding. In the two hours we were at the salon, I guess the weather had amped it up quite a bit in the process.

Four mimosas deep and still hadn't eaten anything, Beth and I hopped in the car and headed to grab a quick bite to eat before the ceremony. Well, quick is not what happened.

Our ceremony was supposed to begin at five and we were still stuck at McDonalds at 5:15. Oops. Juan rang Beth to let her know that he too was running late. Finally, after another twenty minutes had passed, I was told eleven of our twelve guests had arrived and that my future hubby was already waiting down the aisle for me.

I threw another quick layer of my butterscotch lipstick on, tightened my gold heel strap, and wrapped my arm between Gary's.

What happened next was a beautiful, absolutely perfect declaration of two crazy love birds wanting to spend their lives together with the help and commitment from God.

After nine months of being together, we couldn't wait another second before declaring our love in front of God and our closest family and friends. We floated down the aisle after saying *I Do* and jumped right into my two-wheel VW into the snowstorm for our wedding day pictures.

Alongside our photographer, we arrived at *our park* to take outdoor pictures in four inches of snow, while I was wearing a t-length gown and a makeshift sweater bought from Urban Outfitters. Our noses were red, snow was on our shoes, my lipstick had faded, and yet they are the most precious memories that I have. Looking back, I don't remember the temperature. I don't remember if I was cold. All I remember is the look in Juan's eyes and the way he held me so tight.

Side note: It's incredible how smooth and easy everything was, especially on such a tight deadline. Sure, it was a bit tense not knowing all the details in advance, but isn't that life? God is always trying to take that control back into His rightful hands, saying "Hey, remember me? I've got this! Release, child!"

Our wedding was unique in many ways, just like our relationship. And, that is our story. *That* is the story that we could tell our future children and grandchildren. *That* is a story where God gets all the glory! Can I get an amen?

* *

I had just graduated college with my bachelor's in communications and a minor in fashion. People kept asking me what my plan was, and I would confidently say, "I'm going to work for Pronovias in New York!"

After going to Barcelona, I was especially driven to work for them at their grand showroom in Manhattan. My husband and I had a plan; we were going to work our butts off for five months to be able to move us halfway across the country and afford a life in the big apple.

I was waitressing part-time as well as working as a bridal consultant so financially, it seemed like a relatively achievable plan, especially alongside Juan's full-time construction job. After five months, we had saved up just enough money to make it all happen.

The dream was always to move to New York, but knowing that we didn't quite have the means to sustain a mid-rise apartment on the Upper East side meant that we settled for New Jersey.

We started researching apartments in Jersey, while having no context to pricing, proximity to the city, or safe neighborhoods. We ended up finding a beautiful three-bedroom apartment online, only fifteen minutes from the city. We got in touch with the realtor, Skyped to see the apartment, and decided that this was the one. We were so busy packing, tying up loose ends, and planning going away parties, that the last thing we focused on were the details of the house we had selected.

So, off we went. We hopped in a U-Haul with a fraction of our things, our car towed behind us, and hit the road. We drove a straight thirteen hours to see my dad and Beth at the halfway point in Ohio before getting back on the road to New Jersey.

Carrie Bradshaw, here I come!

*It's really happening, God! We did it! *

Love Found Its Way

The GPS revealed that we were seven minutes away. As we were looking around, Juan skeptically let out, "Hmm, this area doesn't look very nice."

Optimistically, I gleamed, "Well, we're not there yet. I'm sure we're just in a small radius that is gentrifying."

*Thank you, Lord, for always letting me see things the way you do, even though I look extremely naïve to the rest of the world! *

Blocks and blocks continued and to everyone's surprise, it did not get better. Trash littered the sidewalks, stores were boarded up during business hours, and clear drug dealings happened every third block.

We pulled up to our new apartment building, just enthused to have made it after such a long journey. We parked the U-Haul in a tight parallel spot in front of our new five story brick home to get a first peak at our apartment. We walked four flights up, opened the door, and fell in love. The apartment was beautiful. It was a spacious three-bedroom apartment with a living room, dishwasher, and full maple hardwood throughout. We shrieked over finding the deal of a lifetime and decided to overlook the location, especially because it was dark as we drove by. After taking everything in, we hurried back to our truck to begin unloading.

At this point we were fighting against the clock as the U-Haul had to be returned by 7pm and we still had a fully loaded truck at 5:30. Exhausted, Juan and I tag-teamed, taking everything out of the U-Haul as quickly as our arms would allow, and walked up the creaky steps into our new apartment.

Only by God's grace were we able to accomplish moving our entire bed, couch, and boxes within forty-five minutes. I wish we had a picture from this moment because my face was as red as an apple and Juan had sweat through every piece of clothing he was wearing. But the race wasn't over; we still needed to return the U-Haul truck by 7:30 or we would get charged an additional day, all before the buzzer timed out.

We drove NASCAR-style, rushing to the U-Haul location. Pulling in at 7:27, we just made the cut-off. It was 7:30 by the time that the paperwork got checked back in and we removed our car from the dolly. We jumped into our cramped navy Passat and headed back to our new oasis.

As we were driving back, we told ourselves, "It's dark out. I'm sure it'll look different in the morning."

*Such cute naivety. Thanks God! *

We stopped at the first Chinese take-out restaurant we saw on the corner off JFK Blvd before heading back home. As we were holding each other amidst the sweat and tears, we were just so happy and proud that we made it.

We ordered two portions of Beef Lo Mein and proceeded back to our new home. That night we decided we wouldn't take anything out of boxes, so instead, we sat on our kitchen floor with the napkins and silverware they provided, and our water bottles, while scarfing our late-night dinner.

****

At the end of our year in Greenville (Google it, I dare you), we were laughing looking back at how dangerous the area really was, with reports of gun violence and gangs, blocks from where we were living.

When we first moved to the area, Juan and I would walk down JFK to bodegas, realizing that people on the streets were eyeing us up and down, and yet, we never felt threatened.

Weekly, I went to the laundromat, and there would always be a clump of men on the street who would catcall me, mostly by gifting me the nickname "Snowflake." It was an interesting time, yet all we could see was the excitement of being in Manhattan every weekend.

*That's the funny thing about God; If you pray strategically, He will reveal places how He wants you to see it, not how the world wants you to. God kept us in this naïve Minnesotan bubble because regardless of all the sketchy-like situations, we never felt unsafe. All praise be to God. *

During our time in Jersey City, we were always on the search for a new home church. We would spend each week going to different churches, hoping to find the right fit. We would Google: "new-age," "Christian," "contemporary," and we would go try them out, hoping to find our new home base.

We had some interesting encounters at these churches. We had experienced the pushy Christians who wanted our first born, social security number, and full story for admittance, and others where we were completely ignored, as if we didn't fit the mold.

Months later, the search continued. We decided to drive into Hoboken, which was a town about thirty minutes away, and rumor had it that it was drastically nicer.

We were driving on the main downtown road and instantly fell in love. You could see that this town was family friendly, had lots of young people walking around, a wide mix of ethnicities, dogs, and an overall sense of enjoyment. We decided to park the car and walk around to better see what this town had to offer.

Hoboken is right on the other side of the Hudson and has the most majestic view of Manhattan. With rosé parties on the piers and young people biking everywhere, we were hooked. We were walking around aimlessly when we came to a street sign for a church that read, "We don't just live here. We love here." Based on that sign, we decided that come the following Sunday, we would check it out.

When Sunday came, I put on my cherry plum lipstick and dressy shirt, excited to see what this Hoboken church was going to be like. Twenty minutes in, we knew this was the one for us.

****

At this point, Juan and I still had made no friends on the East Coast but were eager to break into some groups. On the third Sunday we attended this hip church, hosted in an auditorium, the pastor gave a message about the power of testimonies.

He went on to say, "If anyone feels as if they are being called to go up to the third floor after service to give your testimony, there will be someone waiting for you by the elevator."

The service finished and as Juan was grabbing his second handful of powdered donuts, I said, "I'll be right back babe. I'm going to go upstairs."

Wiping the powder off his lips, Juan muffled, "Why?"

"I feel as if this is what I am supposed to do. I'll be back soon. Go mingle!"

*That's one of my favorite things about being in relationship with Christ; the Holy Spirit! The Holy Spirit guides you with *feelings* and *nudges* and because of free will, He sits back to see if you'll listen to the Holy Spirit, regardless of understanding the vision. So incredibly cool. *

I got into the elevator with a woman who had a beautiful smile and was quick to chat. After introducing ourselves, I told Rachel that my husband and I just moved here, were brand new to the church and by the Holy Spirit, I felt called to give my testimony. Rachel responded with a look of love saying that she too felt called to do it but was scared because she had never done anything like this before.

As we were waiting to be brought into the filming room, Rachel told me about her weekly all-female dinner group. Rachel oversaw a dinner group where other females from the church met up once a week to talk about the sermons, while enjoying each other's company and catching up on life. She said they were having their next group on Monday (the day after) and she would love it if I joined.

Quickly after, a young gentleman came into the hallway, quickly glanced at me and uttered, "Alright, are you ready?"

I followed him into a classroom where there were lights, one oversized camera, and a crew of three people all pointing directly at the spotlight reflecting off the wooden stool. They briefed me beforehand with what they were looking for and said, "Okay, let's do this!" I took a deep breath and let God put the sentences together.

Five minutes later, I walked out of that room feeling on fire for God. (It can be found on YouTube under "Erica's Story".) I went downstairs to find Juan and to tell him all about the girl I had met, the invite to go to a dinner group, and the recording I did. The next day, I decided to take a chance and go follow God's coincidental interaction I had with Rachel.

As I hit the button to bring me up to the seventh floor in this swanky high-rise apartment off the Hudson, I headed into a stranger's home, anxious to see what the night would bring. I was welcomed by eight women of all different ages, professions, and lifestyles.

I had the time of my life. I never felt intimidated or shy as I had other times when doing things for my faith; instead, I knew that I had just met some of my newest best friends.

There was one girl in particular that I felt a strong connection with. Her name was Ilene. Ilene was an amazon-like gorgeous blonde who was freshly engaged. She had a sass to her that really aligned with my sense of humor, so I quickly knew we'd hit it off.

After the first dinner group, I stayed behind to chat more with her and offer any help I could with her upcoming engagement. The following week, I stayed behind again to further get to know her and before I knew it, we had exchanged numbers and made margarita plans (my kind of girl).

It didn't take long before all eight of those girls became my very close friends and through other connection events at church, my friend base was becoming better than ever. After hearing about how much I was clicking with others in Hoboken, Juan decided to join an all-male dinner group where he too made many new friends and found a safe spot to share about his questions and thoughts about his new found relationship with Christ.

After finding this new church home in Hoboken but still living in Jersey City, we had decided that once our lease was up, we had to make the move. When the time came, we started searching for apartments in Hoboken, finding a place in the town center with a great rent price.

Being that Hoboken is one mile, we decided to sell the trustworthy Volkswagen and commit to our new home.

* *

I worked with Pronovias for a few months as one of their top sales professionals. It was an enriching experience of learning about sales techniques for different personality types as well as having the financial opportunity to collect commission off a $15,000 dress.

I loved Pronovias and learning about their processes, but something I didn't enjoy was the cattiness within the retail space. If I sold well that day, I was torn down. If I had a question, I was ignored. There was a popularity scale that management went off, and I clearly never received the handbook. To spare you the details, I needed to make a switch for my own emotional sanity. Meanwhile, Juan got a job one month after me, working for a construction company in the city.

Very quickly after I stopped working for Pronovias, I got hired at The Knot working in advertising sales. The Knot was a great company to work for and taught me a lot during the year I worked for them. I had only graduated a few months prior, and I was still figuring out what I liked and craved in a job. After selling bridal dresses in a retail setting for six years, I was sure that I wanted to make a switch to a 9-5 setting and gain my weekends back.

The Knot was the perfect transition for college graduates because this company knows how to party. Every week they had a Thirsty Thursday in their lounge as well as many other bonding type events throughout the month. I soaked up as much information as I could but ultimately walked out of that job feeling like culturally, I wasn't a fit. I needed creativity, getting my hands dirty, fixing problems, and doing many different tasks during my day, all of which I wasn't offered. While I was working for XO Group, I made sure to really research what my next step should have been.

I was all hopped up on entrepreneurship around that time as I was listening to podcasts, watching every episode of *Shark Tank*, and reading as many books as Amazon would ship. My goal was to become efficient, make the right connections, and go after my dreams.

One episode of *Shark Tank* that really stuck out to me was a Midwestern girl who moved to NYC to pursue her bridal dreams by starting her own business selling bridal gowns online at a reduced price. I was convinced that Samantha from Nearly Newlywed and I were going to be best friends; she just didn't know it yet.

After working for The Knot, I got really tech savvy, specifically finding out details about companies and contacts. I wanted to know more about Samantha, so I started scrolling through her website and transitioned over to her social accounts. I found her personal email and reached out to her with who I was and why she needed to know me.

It wasn't the first time I reached out so boldly, in fact, I did this with Kleinfeld's, Pronovias, and Cowspiracy (the Netflix documentary that turned me to veganism years later.)

Samantha was quickly interested in me, my resume, and the connections we had in common. We set up a meeting a few weeks down the road to meet at The Wing near Gramercy. The connection we had was undeniable. I felt like for the first time in my life, I was having an actual business meeting where we were focused on being empowered women and inspiring each other through what we wanted out of our careers. We had so much in common and I was just in awe that God orchestrated the meeting so easily.

*Thank you, Jesus! *

I was still working for The Knot but was in talk with Samantha about a position becoming available on her team in the near future. I wanted to make sure that I wasn't going to put all my eggs in the one Nearly Newlywed basket though, so I kept my eyes and ears open.

At this point in my life, my heart was yearning for something more, something involving God. I wasn't sure if I was supposed to continue the path of bridal or find something more in line with God's work but in one particular moment, it became crystal clear.

During Sunday morning announcements, Sandy was talking about the opportunities available at the church, saying if we had any desires in our hearts, then we should look into them and apply.

As soon as I got home, I hopped on their website to see what positions were available. On the computer screen, the role flashed, "Communications Director." My heart lit up! I went to school for communications and have had many roles where I had to go out into the community to gauge people's interest for a cause. Within moments, I was applying for the job and praying that God would take over.

Days later, I received an email from the Pastor's assistant, inviting me to an interview. I was overwhelmed by the idea of working for the church. I prayed constantly leading up to the interview.

Lord God, what an incredibly cool opportunity. I am grateful for the chance to be a part of something bigger. Regardless of whether this position is made for me or not, I ask that you allow me to find joy. I would love this job, so Lord, I ask that you would be with me through the interview process and take over where my shortcomings are. But, if this job isn't never meant for me, remind me that you have something better in store. Thank you, Father God. I love you and I pray in your son's beautiful name. Amen.

God carried through, like always. The interview with the pastor was great and I was told that they would keep in touch about next steps.

I was called in for another interview where I met with two people from the worship team, Sam and Matt. After that, I was brought in for a third interview with the assistant Pastor in which I found out it was between myself and one other person. Sure enough, the church ended up picking the other candidate.

When I found the news out, I felt perfectly content and at peace.

*Wow, God! You sure came through on that prayer. You surely must have something better in store, if it's not this. *

I thanked God for giving me the opportunity and teaching me the things He did on the journey. From that, I declared I was going to get back into the bridal industry. It was clear, at least for the moment, that I was going to stay working in bridal so I figured it would be best to see a different side that I hadn't yet...a wedding venue.

I hoped on TheKnot.com to check out venues in New York. I came across a few venues that I thought fit my vision: family owned, respectably sized, and had its own in-house catering. I found a cute rustic warehouse in Brooklyn and decided to reach out to them with:

Hello there,
My name is Erica Hedtke Barreto. I am reaching out to you because I think your party spaces are BEAUTIFUL! I have been working in the bridal industry for over six years and am extremely interested in switching over to a venue! I currently work for The Knot. I can see not only your beautiful venue but also, how well you're received with your local brides!
I'm not sure if you are currently hiring; however, I would be very interested in an event or sales position. If anything opens, I would love to be considered!

Thank you very much for your time and I hope you're enjoying your holiday season!
EHB

One day later I received an email saying that it was so funny I reached out because they were just discussing internally that they were looking to find someone who had bridal and sales experience.

*Funny how this keeps happening to me! Is it because I trusted that inner voice, aka The Holy Spirit? Big 'ol YUP. *

The following Friday, I was invited for an interview at their gorgeous re-built garment factory, and with Jesus' blessing, I accepted the position they offered, on the spot.

I was brought on as an Events Director who handled all events from start to finish as well as coordinated their social accounts.

As for Samantha from Nearly Newlywed, we stayed in touch and I prayfully asked how our relationship would circle back.

* *

While I was searching for my next direction, Juan was doing the same thing. He graduated as a civil engineer in Venezuela, but it was extremely difficult to go work in that field without re-entering grad school for the exact same degree he already had.

Around the time, not only was I hitting it hard with reading materials and self-improvement resources, but so was Juan.

This led us to go to a one-day entrepreneur conference in Brooklyn. Unbeknownst to us, this was a conference about investing in real estate. Now for me, I was sitting back thinking it was a scam, but by the look on Juan's face, you would have thought the Lord Jesus came floating down over that stage.

We left that conference with a binder full of notes and what I could sense was a large conversation on the horizon. Juan and I grabbed brunch nearby at this trendy little corner spot off North 10th to talk through our thoughts about the conference.

It was clear to me that Juan's mind was racing because whenever he has a lot on his mind, he is literally speechless.

I brought up my thoughts about real estate and investing and transitioned the conversation to ask, "what did you think of it all?"

Juan turned slightly in his chair as if he would be making a lot of hand gestures. "Babe, I want to do this."

"Okay. What does that mean? Which part?"

"I want to go into real estate. The long-term plan would be investing but for right now, this is perfect. This way I will learn the sales side to the industry. Eventually, I want to own a construction company, so this just makes sense."

"Alright babe. Let's do it!"

And that about sums up our relationship. I will support my husband's dreams with a 100% backing system if the same support is duplicated for me.

So, Juan dove right in. Within three months of that conference, he took his certification, became licensed, and signed up with Citi Habitats.

Following God's Given Path

Fast forward six months later and real estate wasn't panning out the way we had hoped for Juan. He would come home frustrated that clients weren't returning his calls. He would have multiple no-show appointments with deals unraveling, left and right.

Knowing when it's time to call it, Juan threw in his towel. While we waited to hear from God about His next move, we were depending on my income to support us. We vowed from that moment on that we weren't going to let finances get in the way of our marriage or our attitudes.

During this time, we learned to really lean on God with our finances and knew we needed to be consistent with tithing. After hearing testimony after testimony from my parents about how God really shined in their lives when it came to money, we took the leap and gave the topic of finances over to God. We decided to give ten percent of my income back to God and sometimes more when we felt it in our hearts.

Even though you would think times would be tough with two people living off one salary and giving away ten percent of it, it never seemed that way. There were a few months we were tight on our rent but like Jesus-instant-rice, our families would help us make up what we were missing or we would randomly get a check in the mail for the exact amount we needed.

*I don't know about you, but tithing is such an incredible opportunity to bless your faith families all over the world AND show God your commitment to Him! *

As we were really pulling back on going out, hanging out with our friends, and date nights, we did want to do something special for our anniversary that was coming up the following March.

I was still working with the wedding venue and things were going swimmingly well. I had just gotten a raise, which came at the perfect time, and I was feeling really valued in my role.

One particular Wednesday, I had an appointment to meet up with a local hotel to talk about a partnership opportunity. The hotel was wanting us to recommend them as accommodations, while in exchange, wanted some of those out of state travelers to choose us as their destination wedding or dinner spot. I was super excited for the meeting because it was a beautiful, very Brooklyn-chic hotel in Williamsburg.

Waiting at an overly trendy copper table, an exotic concierge from Russia, came over to talk to me about her ideas of the collaboration. We instantly clicked and I knew that a good partnership was forming. Through the conversation, it became apparent that we may have had the upper hand, so before our meeting ended, I casually asked if the employees of my venue could stay at the hotel for free, as a perk to the agreement.

She thought for a second and said, "Yes! If it's Monday-Thursday, that is fine!"

Fast acting, I pushed one step further and said, "Amazing! Well...I do have an anniversary coming up, but it's on a Friday...."

Without skipping a beat, she went on, "Oh, I'm sure that's fine! Email me the dates and I'll confirm it!"

A day later, I received a confirmation email from Rifka confirming that we were going to stay Friday night for our anniversary!

*Such a blessing! Thank you, God! Who knew He cared about such small things, like my anniversary! *

With our anniversary in mind, we were still racking our brains as to how we could make a little extra cash to go out to dinner that night. Well like a Jesus Easy-bake oven, our prayers were answered.

We were heading over to our best friends' house to hang out with Rico and Sylvia and their two beautiful kids. We were having fun making pasta, playing Wii with the kids, and drinking wine.

Through conversation, we mentioned how we really wanted to go out to dinner for our anniversary but chirped, "it's fine, we'll probably make a lovely dinner at home, instead."

Rico, always clever with his ideas, added, "I can get you guys a reservation at the restaurant I work at! More than that, I can give you the friends and family discount!"

Rico worked for one of the nicest steakhouses in midtown, the type of place you wouldn't dare step into unless you were wearing designer from head to toe. Completely taken back by the generosity, we said yes, but in the back of our minds told ourselves that there was a chance we wouldn't make the reservation, due to the foreseen bill size.

*Complete blessing nonetheless! *

A few days later after hard days of work with temperamental brides, I let loose with one of my girlfriends in her two-bedroom Hoboken condo. We shared a few glasses of wine and deep conversation about things on our minds. I mentioned that times were a bit tight but how God was really providing.

After a few hours and too much wine, I told her that I ought to head home. I slid my grey Ugg boots on when she told me to hang tight for a moment. She ran into her room down the long hallway, came back out, and handed me $120. She told me that her parents had given it to her for "no reason" and how she was perfectly fine without it. She continued that she wanted Juan and me to have a great anniversary, and with some resistance to her selfless generosity, I was on my way.

****

It was the day of our anniversary and God had provided for us in incredible ways.

After work, we both commuted home back to Hoboken, changed into fancy duds, and went back into Manhattan for our dinner reservation.

We strolled into Morton's Steakhouse around seven and was elated by the occasion. As we were being led to our table, we were in awe, taking in the gorgeous lighting and fancy guests seated near our table. The maître d' placed our open menus in front of us and as we glanced down, we felt overwhelmed at how little we understood about meat cooking techniques and aged processes.

Thankfully, Rico was working, so he walked us through what we should order, along with taking the liberty of ordering our drinks and asparagus appetizer. The whole meal was delicious, and the drinks were endless. Truly, I lost count.

When the bill came, Juan and I clutched hands as we knew we ate and drank far more than what we could afford. We glanced down with one eye open and saw a total of $102.

Completely out of words, we pulled our friend aside and said, "Rico!! You didn't charge us for all of those drinks or the appetizers!"

In his suave accent, he said, "It's on me, my friends! Happy anniversary!"

*Are you kidding me?! So, we tithed and trusted our money over to God, and THIS is how He blesses us back?! What an incredible God we get to call Father! *

After dinner, we floated over to the chic hotel in Brooklyn. We checked in at the front desk with the very straight-faced man with a tie and headed toward the elevator. We checked into a beautifully modern apartment with a glass shower, fully stocked liquor cabinet, sound machine, and plush robes.

We laughed at how incredible the whole day had been, falling onto the bed, laughing over the craziness of the day. It was a beautifully perfect day, completely shadowed by God's love for us.

Born again

My best friend, Olivia, was in town and per her request, we went out to the local bars until bar close and beyond. Let me preface by saying that I'm not one to love to do this.

Saturday night, we found ourselves in a group with Juan, Olivia, me, and two random men who happened to tag along, clearly gunning for Olivia. Slugging around downtown Hoboken from spot to spot, Juan and I were getting sleepy and oh, so ready to head home. However, we knew we couldn't leave Olivia in a town she hardly knew, with men no one knew. So, we stayed.

We all stepped outside of the madness of 20 somethings trying to get a little something-something, for some fresh air and a smoke. Olivia and the two guys wanted a quick drag for the umpteenth time of the night, as we stood between this dive bar and a raggedy diner.

Casually standing outside in our group of five, a younger guy strolled up to us and asked if we had an extra smoke. This man, appearing to be in his twenties, seemed to be as harmless as they come.

Alex had salt and pepper hair, monochromatic grey clothes, and a whole lot of baggage. I mean that quite literally. Alex had a crutch for his unstable right leg and a beat-up black suitcase. I admired his spirit as he came up to a group of complete strangers with no fear.

As we asked innocent questions like, "What is your name" and "Where are you off to," he sounded like he wanted to join us at the diner.

We all went into the diner, with Olivia making out with bachelor number one in the booth, and the rest of us sitting at the traditional bar stools, waiting to be served. The random gentleman number two, gunning for my friend, proceeded to order breakfast with his slurred words. We ordered a side of sweet potato fries to split and asked our new addition, Alex, if he was going to get anything.

Meek, he responded, "I don't have any money."

Immediately, Juan jumped in without hesitation, "Are you hungry? If so, order. It's on us."

Sure enough, he ordered and it wasn't one of those, *I'm really hungry but I'll just order a water and side item;* instead, he ordered himself a big 'ol breakfast platter full of bacon, sausage, pancakes, eggs, and toast.

Sitting at the counter, we found out more about Alex. He shared that he lost his job a few months ago, was newly divorced and kicked out of his home, someone stole his cell phone & wallet, his ID expired (not that it mattered because it was stolen), and he fell and sprained his kneecap. If this wasn't a modern-day Job, I don't know what is!

Side note: If you haven't read the book of Job in the Old Testament, I highly encourage you! It's a relatively short book, jam packed with action, plot twists, and incredible take-aways!

Entranced by everything he was saying, he added, "I've really just been jumping around from couch to couch with my belongings. Some days I go to the homeless shelter, which is smelly and filled with a lot of negativity. Other times, I walk around through the night, just hoping to get a bed for the following day. People are really nice and help me with food, just like you guys. It's a really hard situation to be in and even harder to get out. I've gone to all the government offices to try to reinstate my license, but I can't without proper paperwork, money, and an ID, which I don't have. It's hard for me to get a job without a cell phone or computer." And believe me...it went on.

Stunned by his tenacity and lack of bitterness through everything he was going through, we asked, "Well, where are you staying tonight?"

"I don't know yet. I was initially hoping the shelters would have open spots for tonight, but they're all full. Most likely I'm just going to roam around all night and hope I get a spot tomorrow."

*Something stirred, not just in my heart, but in Juan's, when we met Alex. We knew we needed to be a part of his story; we just didn't know how. *

Sitting in the diner and praying that the night could come to an end, I turned toward Juan with big puppy eyes and him staring right back at me with a full heart.

We pivoted towards Alex and pleaded, "Come stay with us tonight. If you don't mind sleeping on our floor, we'd be happy to have you."

Alex became teary eyed and innocently inquired, "Why are you guys so nice?"

I opened my mouth and God let out the words. "Because this is what Christ would have done."

*That was the second time God has spoken through me and it absolutely blew me away. *

We proceeded all the way home as a group of four, leaving behind the two horndogs who so badly wanted the night to end with a hot little toddy, nestled in their bed.

We had to switch up our living arrangements a bit; Olivia was now sleeping with me in our queen size bed, while Juan took the Ikea pull-out couch in our living room. Alex slept on the floor in the living room; all in our cramped 600 square foot apartment.

In the morning, Alex quickly gathered his things to leave, as we were about to begin making pancakes and bacon. We asked what he had planned for the day and where he was going to stay for the next night.

He had a full itinerary planned, trying to get his ID reinstated, a government issued cell phone and find some food throughout the day.

Before he left, I gave him both Juan and my cell phone numbers and told him that if he didn't find somewhere to sleep that night to call us and again, he could sleep on our floor.

The day passed and nighttime came, and we received a phone call from Alex. He told us that all the beds at the shelter were taken and asked if he could stay with us that night. We happily agreed.

Olivia was heading back to Minnesota the next morning, so we said our goodbyes and proceeded to ask Alex again what his plans were for sleeping arrangements. He came over the next night as well, now transitioning to our grey pull-out couch.

Juan and I had exchanged a few words in secret that night and ultimately came to the conclusion that God simultaneously asked both of us to watch over Alex. The next night when Alex stayed with us, we told him the good news.

"Alex, if you want, we would be happy for you to stay with us while you get back on your feet."

Alex became very silent and his eyes filled with tears. "I don't know why you guys are doing this, but thank you so much."

For two months, we had the pleasure of getting to know Alex. Like, really get to know him because again, we lived in a tiny one-bedroom apartment. He left his items in our living room, showered, ate breakfast, snacks and dinner with us, received resume help, applied for jobs on our laptops, used our transportation cards for job interviews, and even accompanied us to church.

Weekly, he would leave during the day while we went to work and then return around dinner time. I so enjoyed our conversations at night because he would become vulnerable, asking questions of faith and pondering who this Jesus guy was. Alex was a proclaimed agnostic, but his hunger to know who Christ was unbreakable.

He asked some really hard questions. Now I don't claim to know everything; Lord knows I am very wrong about a lot of things, especially such a gigantic topic as faith, but I did my best to answer questions based on scripture.

We invited Alex to church for two weeks before he finally gave into the pressure, and came with the understanding that he would get free donuts, bagels, and orange juice.

On our first visit going as a threesome, we went right to the front row, just as we normally would, and praised, sang, and listened intently to the message about forgiveness. After the service, we introduced him to all our friends and members of the church.

The next Sunday, he asked if he could join us at church "for the killer music and donuts."

After each service, we would walk home and talk about what we thought of the message, which was always fascinating hearing his perspective. Alex's hunger for who Jesus was, why He treated people with such love and kindness, regardless of their position in life, really left an imprint on him. Alex would often say how he saw a light and a lot of Jesus-qualities in us, which is incredibly flattering, considering he hardly knew Jesus before he came to stay with us.

The short experience with Alex was so much greater than just letting a stranger stay with us. This was the way in which Christ would reveal himself to Alex. The Lord chose to use Juan and I because of the compassion we have for the homeless.

What Alex loved about us, so he said, was the way we didn't seem like other Christians.

See, Alex was under the impression that a Christian was judgmental, had their nose stuck up in the air, and never dared to sin, but was quick to point out others'. But through our relationship with Alex, we showed him that though we can all have those tendencies (Christian or non-Christian), our goal is to shine through life with love and kindness, similar to our Lord and Savior, giving up judgement and hate.

Alex was smitten by the way Juan and I lived, as Christians. He was blown away by who this God was that we imitated and lived our life alongside of. He would continuously ask the same questions, trying to better understand our intentions and hearts.

Alex made it clear, he didn't understand why we did everything that we did. He didn't get why we were so accepting to a stranger coming into our home and how we were so trusting and forgiving when his white lies would be exposed. He didn't understand how Jesus was the sole reason behind us doing this. He also, on repeat, questioned what we wanted in return.

Whenever we said, "Nothing Alex. We simply want to love on you and give you a chance when no one else would, because that's the kind of thing Jesus would do."

Alex was completely taken off-guard. Like I said, he thought Christians were all stuffy with lots of rules like "Don't drink, don't swear, do this for me, then, I'll do this for you..." Unfortunately, this is a big stereotype for what people think Christians are. And I'm not saying that these types of Christians don't exist, because they do, but that is not who Christ was.

To be a Christian is to be a Christ follower. If you follow Christ, you choose to live the way He lived: selfless, loving, showing kindness and generosity. As followers of Christ, we go off what the Bible says, but when people start twisting the Bible to align with their own positioning and thoughts, that's when Christians can be led astray.

A great example was when we opened a bottle of wine on a Friday night. He was totally thrown off and would say things like, "Wait...are you allowed to do that?"

That opened a beautiful opportunity to explain sin and what Jesus did for us on the cross, allowing us to stay in our sin and obtain free will.

I explained that being a Christian doesn't mean you are perfect or are expected to be. However, when Christians sin, they feel **convicted** of those sins, and actively turn from them, trying to be more Christ-like moving forward.

****

Occasionally we would get invited to game nights hosted by our friends and with permission, we would invite Alex along. It was incredible seeing Alex's confidence get re-built through meeting new friends and being encouraged to let loose.

After almost two months, we decided it was time for Alex to flap those wings and fly, because did I mention that we were living in a tiny apartment for three grown adults, and on one salary?

To this day we still talk. We are so grateful for the experience we shared together and how God used all of us in this unique testimony.

Not only did Alex's time with us, leave a huge imprint on our hearts, but it left a ripple effect on a whole community.

Almost everyone in church found out that we were hosting a homeless man and for no reason other than, to be obedient to the Holy Spirit. This touched people's hearts as it helped them better understand how God moves, in real time. It touched our hearts and added yet another beautifully rich example of God's love. Lastly, it affected a non-believer, Alex, and isn't that the whole point of this thing called life?

Alex may not have given himself over to Jesus at that time, but I can confidently say that he started his journey with us, and God won't stop working until his soul is claimed.

In the Bible, there is a parable saying that we can help plant the seed, but then someone else might take it over to water, prune it, and so on. Our mission isn't always to bring that person from A to Z in their relationship with Christ; simply planting the seed is a remarkable step that allows the plant to bloom. And as Christians, that is a huge win!

All In

After having gone through such a wild ride, Juan and I were on fire for Christ and wondering what was next. We were both active in our church with weekly attendance, volunteering, and participating in dinner groups. I also sang in the choir and Juan was a part of the building crew. Still, we ached for more. Little did I know how God was going to challenge me.

My stepmom, Beth, and I do Bible study every Wednesday around six o'clock. Five minutes prior to our call, I went into my room and opened my Bible to Esther, as I jumped onto my plush teal comforter.

I answered the phone and I sensed something different in her voice right away. After a few minutes of asking how I was, she paused for what seemed like three minutes and said, "Erica, I'm so sorry, but your dad and I are getting divorced."

I kept the phone to my right ear while she was talking, but my head was spinning, face flushed with wet tears and blurred vision.

She continued on that my dad cheated on her throughout their ten-year marriage and there was no way to repair the trust.

Feeling betrayed on so many levels, she brought me back by reassuring me that this wouldn't change a thing between us and how she wanted more than anything for me to remain in her life.

Bible study didn't happen that week and when we got off the phone, I sat feeling numb, thinking about everything she said. I sat and thought about how they had acted together when we visited that July for my stepbrother's high school graduation.

In a way, I was completely surprised and caught off guard because they had appeared to be head over heels for ten years. But on the other hand, there were a lot of warning signs.

Rumor had it that my dad had cheated on my mom. I hadn't quite known why stepmom number two didn't work out. Maybe, it also had to do with a wondering eye. But Beth? She is like the modern-day Mother Theresa! My stomach was in knots, knowing that my dad wouldn't find a better woman than Beth.

After that call, I swallowed my own feelings, and knew I had to be strong for Beth. Her world had just shattered, catching her completely off guard, and the last thing she needed to think about was where our relationship was going to stand. I vowed from that night forward that I would be her rock.

I called her every day, making sure she was okay. I listened. I cried with her. I sent her flowers. I bought a plane ticket just to hug her while she cried. I did anything I could to show her that our love was unbreakable and that having my dad in the mix didn't define our relationship.

As for my dad, he was a total mystery. He was still with his mistress and apparently head over heels, ready to get down on one knee. I had to walk a fine line between loving him unconditionally but also, not condoning his behavior. It was an awkward spot that I'd never been in before with him; one where I held the moral compass.

For the first time in my life, I finally felt like the veil had been lifted. I quickly pieced together that everything about him was a façade. I wasn't sure if I knew the real him or just the guy he projected to be.

His marriage had come to an end and on a human level, I wanted to make sure he was doing okay.

On the second phone call I had with him since the announcement of the divorce, he told me the 'real reasons' for the divorce but never once admitted the infidelity.

Something in me snapped. "Dad! Enough is enough. I'm sick and tired of all the lies. We either have a real relationship filled with the truth or we don't have one at all. I know everything. I know what you did, and I know you're the reason your marriage failed."

Long moments separated us and softly I heard, "Okay, you're right."

From that moment on, he vowed to have an honest relationship with me, even if things would be difficult to say.

Months later, Beth slowly came back to life, like an animated character at Chuck E Cheese. Her church family was a big part of it, as well as my two stepbrothers.

Above all, she leaned heavy on God, needing His grace to pick up her broken pieces. Through His eyes, she was reminded of her significance and that it stood independent of others.

Beth's faith was strengthened in such a beautiful way that joy is the only word I can use to sum up her transformation. Through the year-long process, she became a beautiful, wide-winged angel, even brighter than the one she was before.

Feeling so inspired by Beth's courage and strength, I knew it was time to take the next step in my faith, quite literally.

It was a beautiful Sunday in May when I watched one of my close friends get baptized. It was a beautiful declaration that made me cry like a big baby at the step she was taking. Something in my heart stirred and I knew that God was telling me that it was my turn.

*Okay, I'm truly understanding and hearing His prompts clearly now. *

The next month the church was hosting a class discussing what a baptism was. I went into the meeting confident that I was going to get baptized in July (because Beth and I had already arranged a trip in July and I wanted her to be there), but there was one question that I needed answered before the final commitment.

The pastor sat down with the four others in the room, explaining how baptism is the physical symbol of showing re-birth and proclaiming your faith.

When there was a lull in conversation, I raised my hand and said, "I'm just nervous that after I get baptized, I won't be able to live up to that standard of being reborn...."

Nodding heads all around, our pastor went on to say how everything in the past is erased and everything moving forward is leaning on God. Now, you move with the understanding that you are living as Christ lived. Sin is something that we strive to do less of and when we do, we feel convicted and auto correct our actions for the next time around. Being baptized doesn't mean you have transformed into a perfect person; it simply means that you are proclaiming your life to look more like Christ's.

* *

July came rather quickly, and while I was over the moon, I was extremely nervous. The week leading up to the baptism I was on edge, the way a high schooler is when they discover they had breakfast stuck in their front tooth all day and their friends were perfectly content without telling them.

I was thinking silly things, like, 'I need to make sure I plug my nose' and 'who do I hug first when I come up from the water?' Over the phone, I confessed these things to Beth and she gently reminded me that as soon as the day came, all of that would flush away.

Sunday morning finally arrived and I was still feeling shaky, mixed with a side of anxiousness. Still at home, I threw on my navy baptism shirt the church gave me the month before and had Beth, my stepbrother Jack, Juan, and I pray about what was about to happen.

Beth said a beautiful prayer and I was beginning to feel like my nerves were settling slightly. I told everyone I would prefer to head to church alone so I could spend those minutes with God. As I was walking the seven blocks over, I laid it all on the line.

God, I am so excited to be taking this step. I've been wanting to do this for a long time. Thank you for bringing back that nudge and helping this moment be a reality. I can't help but feel nervous, so I just ask for you to wash away those nerves and all the silly thoughts I have. I pray that you would tell the enemy to stand down, as I know that's where all these insecurities are coming from. Let this just be about you. Let this just be about you, Lord God. I love you and I can't wait to see you on the other side. Amen.

I walked into church on Garden Street and instantly felt a beautiful acceptance. Everyone who saw me (and my shirt) congratulated me on the step I was about to make. Within moments, everything I had previously thought melted away. I was instantly reminded, through other people's affirmations, that this step was about God and God, alone. It was 100% God answering my prayers through those words.

*You can't deny that He's really cool, right?! *

After the service concluded, I was instructed to line up along the gymnasium wall and get ready to be called on stage, along with my family and friends.

As the pastor spoke my name into the microphone, everything went a bit hazy. I followed my pastor's cues with where to sit within the tub and what to focus on. I made sure Juan, Beth, and Jack were standing right alongside of me and holding onto me.

As I was sitting in the water, intense emotions started bubbling to the surface. Hardly able to keep it together from the sheer thought of what I was about to confess, the pastor turned to me and asked two questions.

"Erica, is your faith in Christ, and Christ-alone?"

Through tears, I let out, "Yes!" and he continued, "Are you willing to go wherever he leads you?"

"Yes!"

"Then by the confession of your faith and the power vested in me, you are now baptized..."

Without thinking, I pinched my nose, dunked under the water, and came out feeling like a new Erica. I felt symbolically like a snake who had just gotten rid of that icky oily skin and into something new, fresh, and vibrant. I could not contain my feelings and how gigantic my confession felt.

I looked to my left and embraced Juan, wet tee and all, and then went for Beth who held me tighter than she had before. It was the most beautiful moment of my life.

A month later, while talking on the phone with Beth, she confessed how my baptism deeply affected her faith walk—it felt like she too had been re-born and that was also her fresh start, especially after the divorce, an unpleasant diagnosis, and a career change.

My baptism was a beautiful pivot point in my life, and I knew I wanted to keep going on that trajectory in this new chapter as a born-again Christian.

* *

For the past several years, God whispered thoughts and ideas into my head. I would journal these thoughts and testimonies, revealing the ways He constantly pursued me, until eventually it morphed into a book format.

Officially after I got baptized, God had made it clear He wanted me to honestly pursue my writings and put this book of testimonies into the world as an opportunity for others to know who He is. Thus, the book you are reading now was birthed.

Trusting in the Unknown

At this point, I was still working at the wedding venue. I loved my co-workers, but the job itself was starting to take a heavy toll on my heart. I so loved brides and the industry, but every day I felt a stronger and stronger tug on my heart, reminding me of my book. I would try pushing those feelings down by multi-tasking between working at the venue and as a writer at night, but it was beginning to be too hard to juggle. It was almost like I was unsuccessfully walking the opposite direction on those automatic gliders at an airport. I prayed over why I felt such a strong desire to write and what He wanted me to do about the conflict.

Lord, I am so conflicted. You know my heart, Lord God. You know my desire is to serve you. I don't want to feel this ping-pong game anymore. Lord, show me your way and I will follow. If it's writing that you want me to pursue, I'll do it. Simply, show me. I love you, Father God. In Jesus name, Amen.

* *

I was browsing on Facebook one night after work, just seeing what others were up to and what groups I could join to enhance my writing. Jesus was within my computer that Tuesday night because suddenly, I came across a New York best-selling author who was seeking out aspiring authors to help coach. I yelped reading more about her program and sent her a private message right away.

Hi Rachel!

I just saw that you were looking for wanna-be-authors to join your aspiring authors program and I'm very interested! I've been working on a non-fiction book slowly for over two years, but now I truly feel it is the time God wants me to focus on it and send it out into the world! I would love to know more what this program entails!

So excited!
EHB

Within a day, Rachel and I jumped on a call, which was 100% God crafted. This intensive eight-week program gave the aspiring authors tools ranging from brainstorming to marketing to book proposals to launch teams; you name it, she had it!

There were four other girls in the program, all wanting to pursue publishing their own Christian genre books. It was an incredible support group that not only bolstered my writing path but gave me more encouragement than I ever knew I needed.

I am forever grateful of Rachel because to her, she may have been just seeking out a way to bless younger authors, but to me, she was exactly the push I needed to begin making my dreams a reality.

* *

One particularly busy work week, I had been getting strong messages from God. The words "retreat" and "fasting" kept flashing on repeat in my brain. I didn't know what that meant exactly, but I went with my gut feeling as I gracefully sat on the bed next to Juan to let out my next big plan, which is sooo not uncommon in our marriage.

I let out, "Babe, I know this is crazy, but I really feel it on my heart to go away for a long weekend by myself to simply pray, fast, and write."

I went on to say that I needed some quiet space just to focus in on what God was wanting for me but also to hammer out a bulk of writing. With Juan's support, I booked a lake-front room at a cozy resort for the following weekend up at Lake George. And boy, was it magical.

My day consisted of waking up, praying that words would come flowing out of my fingertips, then, (weather permitted) head outside with a blanket over my shoulders and a cup of tea at my side, to begin writing.

I would fast and write the whole day. When my fingers needed a break from typing, I would dive into His Word, get inspired and jump back to my computer.

I had my cell phone off all during the day so there would be no distractions. I made one single phone call to Juan before I went to bed every night, to fill him in on the progress of the day. It was fantastic and I felt so incredibly close to God, as if I was fully hearing what He was whispering into my soul. This trip, literally, topped off my cup.

When I returned home after my trip, I was on fire. Not only did I feel so incredibly close to God after following His steps, but my whole heart and soul was focused on Him through my writing.

Continuing with Rachel's program, I created my own website, really focused on creating content posts, increased my social media following, and having email subscribers that I personally wrote to every week. And though all of this sounds so beautiful, which it was, the enemy scooped in hard, like an eagle spotting a helpless mouse.

The number one thing the enemy wants to do is destroy whatever confidence, support, and tools you have towards your God given gifts. And unfortunately, a lot of the time during the process, it worked.

I would have a down week where I would think, "Who even cares to read what I wrote?" or "I'm not nearly as good of a writer as Donald Miller, so why even bother?"

Then, all of a sudden, my blog posts would come out every two weeks instead of every week. Two weeks turned into three weeks, all because those disgusting whispers in my head drowned out the truth of God.

I know reading that you can go, "Seriously Erica? Why did you listen? You are clearly so gifted," but come on, we have all been there. We've all been there when Satan goes after your most personal, most intimate characteristics and attacks.

"Oh, you think you're a great baseball player?" BOOM, broken arm. "Oh, you think you're a great speaker?" BOOM, you suck and that's why only three people showed up tonight, because remember, you suck.

Seriously, Satan is THE WORST. But truth be told, he is the best at what he does. He convinced me many times that I was less than and that I had no right to even pursue putting my thoughts about God into the world.

But you know what? God will always win. Because sure, I had some confidence shaking here and there, but God won. He constantly reminded me through other people's voices, through writing opportunities, through connections with other authors, that this is what He has planned for me. He has proved time and time again that he is constantly pursuing me. And of course, it makes sense why the enemy wants to interfere...he knows how gifted I am and how I want to use it all to be for the glory of God, so he's going to want to stop that.

Remember that same thing for yourself. Whatever gift God has given you, remember that Satan will try to stop you because if you continue to use it for God, you'll be benefiting His kingdom and Satan's boots shake when that happens.

So... I fought through and dealt with my own battles of what others might be thinking. I fought through the reality that my writing, whether some love it or not, is for God. I fought through rejection. I fought through finances. All to say, it was a very hard spiritual time of attack, but I persevered, or rather, God did.

*God wasn't kidding when He said that there will be tribulations, huh? *

With all my own spiritual rollercoasters that were happening, it was all too much to juggle, alongside a full-time job.

The following day at work, there was a 160-person event at my venue that I oversaw and quite frankly, I was tanking. My brain was so scattered, and I knew that I was letting my team down.

Once the last of the group had left for the evening, I went to go speak to my boss, who was also becoming a great friend. I spilled out my heart to her and confessed, "My heart just isn't here anymore. I really need to focus on this book." And with that, my next chapter as an author was about to open, or so I thought…

The Unexpected

Juan and I decided that while I would be focusing on my writing most of my time, financially, it made the most sense for me to get a part-time job.

As I was hopping from coffee shop to coffee shop raking in all the free Wi-Fi I could, I came across a women's boutique that was looking for a part-time assistant manager. I stopped in and was told by a trendy twenty-year-old to email my resume and cover letter, as I headed back out the door. As I sipped my boujee $5 passion fruit tea at the coffee shop up the block, I began crafting an email to the boutique.

Hi alba boutique!

Let me tell you a little about myself; My name is Erica Barreto and I'm originally from the Midwest. I've been living on the east coast for two years; specifically in Hoboken for one year!

I would love to work for Alba for a few reasons! 1. Alba is the absolute trendiest spot around with the cutest clothes! 2. I love shopping at Alba (even if it's just window shopping!) 3. It's a very close commute to my house 4. Alba in Spanish means Dawn, which is my middle name! Come on, that can't be a coincidence!

Let's set up an interview!
EHB

Literally twenty minutes later, I got an email response back from the owner, Libby, with my interview time.

I was hired right away as their part-time assistant manager.

*Hired on the spot, again? Wow, God is really flinging these doors wide open. *

I was truly loving my new schedule. I had the freedom to be a writer part-time and then hang out with girls all day long, while chatting and casually selling way more clothes than they bargained for, at the boutique. The owners noticed how well I was doing and quickly chatted with me about promoting me to the manager of the store location. I was thrilled with how God had orchestrated all these interactions and plans within my career.

* *

On the personal side of things, Juan and I had been talking about wanting to get pregnant for a few years. We had heard so many comments over a three-year time span. "Why aren't you pregnant yet? Have you tried this? Maybe you should go to the doctor to be checked," and quite frankly, I wasn't having it. I knew without a doubt there was nothing wrong with either one of us and it was truly God's timing for when and if we became a larger family. Feeling so strongly, Juan and I prayed together.

Lord God, please release this topic off our shoulders. It's hard not to get frustrated when others are more concerned about this topic than we are. But Lord, it is because we have full faith in you and your plan for our family. You know the desires in our hearts. You know we would love babies. Ultimately God, we trust that we will be blessed when you say so. Thank you, Jesus, for taking this topic over and softening our hearts to those who don't understand our perspective. I pray over the little angel you may bless us with one day. In your son's Holy name, Lord God, Amen.

* *

After being at Alba for four months or so, I was called into a meeting with my two bosses to receive my first review. I was slightly nervous as to what the feedback was going to be, because from my standpoint, things were going very well with the customer base and my sales numbers.

"So, Erica, we wanted to chat with you about a new opportunity."

They proceeded to tell me that my sales numbers were much higher than any stylist within any of their five locations and asked if I would consider moving into a new role as a sales manager to oversee all of their store locations. I was over the moon. It was a position that already highlighted something I excelled at, and gave me an opportunity to mentor other stylists.

And while the role was awesome, it also came with more responsibility. With it came more distraction. More calls and texts on my time off. More, more, more, which pulled me away from my writing again. But I happily accepted the position and resumed on, doing both writing and selling for this cutie boutique.

Work at Alba was insanely busy with the holidays and I was excited for a break, as we had a lot of company visiting us and another anniversary around the corner.

It was the beginning of the New year and we had Juan's family coming from Miami to visit us. It was their first time coming to the New York area, so of course we showed them all the tourist attractions, our favorite piano bar in Hell's Kitchen, and of course, cozy Hoboken. We had a fabulous time visiting and honestly, it was nice to just have a break from our everyday routines.

A few weeks after the family left, we swept ourselves away to Las Vegas to celebrate our third wedding anniversary. I had pre-booked the trip months in advance, including the Stratosphere hotel, magic show with David Copperfield, and fancy Mediterranean restaurant reservations.

Funny enough, we didn't enjoy Las Vegas very much. We prayed during our trip that God could reveal His vision and His eyes of Vegas, yet all we saw was desperation. We hurt for Vegas. We hurt for the homeless, the wanderers, the desperate. Needless to say, it didn't really give us much of a "let's make a baby" vibe. But we made the most out of the trip.

We walked up and down the strip until my sandals literally broke apart, we ate more guacamole than I should be honest about, and for some reason, I felt it on my heart not to drink during the trip.

I'm not sure why, but it was a small echo in my mind that told me to resist drinking. And so, I did.

*Okay, by now, I know that these voices are from God. I don't always get them or like what they're saying, but I'm going to trust that His thought process is leaps and bounds bigger than mine. *

We returned home after a weekend away and got back to our routines of being a writer and sales manager, and for Juan, working for a construction company in New Jersey. Things were smooth sailing and in a good rhythm.

****

A few weeks later, I was walking to work, and I just felt funny. After moving into a new two-story home, I walked twelve blocks to work every day and back.

For some reason, on this particular morning, I was walking as if I had sand in my panties. Ignoring that strangeness, I got to work, sat at the desk, and continued my opening routines. The next morning when I was walking to work, same thing again.

*Huh.... *

A few evenings later and a few days late (if you get my drift), Juan was still working, and I was pacing.

The enemy was playing mind games with me, reminding me that I have a long line of ovarian cancer in my family, making it nearly impossible for me to get pregnant.

I hopped out of the house for some fresh air and over to the closest CVS. I grabbed a pack of pregnancy tests, as I had so many times in the past. I went home, closed myself into the bathroom, and prayed.

Lord God, I don't know what's going on but just know, I trust your plan. Whatever these results, let me be at peace. Amen.

I unwrapped the white stick, got into my squat position, and aimed, waiting to see if one or two lines appeared. I pulled my pants up, set the stick upside down over the sink, shut the bathroom door behind me, and paced in our living room. Meanwhile, I was praying.

Lord God, I want unshakeable trust and to be reminded that your timing is perfect. Though I would love to be pregnant, I continuously give this up to you. Thank you, Lord God. In Jesus' name, amen.

Five minutes later, because I didn't want the test to know that I was too desperate for the results, I walked into the bathroom, shut the door behind me, took a deep breath, and grabbed the stick.

*Two lines. Damn, not pregnant. Oh wait... two lines? Nope, not pregnant. Dang it. But the box shows two lines as pregnant. WAIT, it has two lines. Does that mean I'm pregnant? Okay, let's not panic, Erica. Go do the second test. *

At this point, Juan still wasn't home and it was about seven at night while I was having all these inner monologues.

I repeated exactly what I did the first time. I peed on the stick, kept the bathroom light on with the door closed, waited six minutes this time, because you know, extra desperate vibes, then went back in.

*Another two lines. Okay, 100% pregnant. *

I paced in our living room for over forty-five minutes, unsure of how to even proceed from there. Juan finally got home, after what felt like twelve days, and I rushed to give him a tight hug. Juan hugged back, shrugging me off quickly to take a shower to remove the caulk from his arms.

Instead, I grabbed his hand and led him to the bathroom, making small talk about our days.

We made it to the bathroom, and I held up the two white and pink pregnancy sticks, showing that we were pregnant. Just like me, he took a few minutes to understand what the two lines meant. Once it sank in, we held each other for minutes, kissing, and crying, imagining what this little one inside of me was like.

Two days later, we made an appointment with the doctor to get everything confirmed and to see how far along I was. It turned out we were five weeks along and we conceived when my in-laws were staying with us (Sorry Tico). Right away, we made a decision not to find out the baby's gender until the day he or she was born.

Being holistic, we also decided that we wanted an all-natural tub birth at a birthing center with midwives by our side.

My mantra while being pregnant was to have nothing but positive energy and avocado mango rolls. And let me tell you, it was an incredible pregnancy. I was glowing seven out of seven days.

I loved being pregnant. I loved feeling my little one roll around. I loved the special attention I got on the subway and in bathroom lines. I loved the excuse of eating what I wanted when I wanted.

Week thirty-nine came, and I was pumped that my little he/she was going to be making their entrance into the world very shortly.

Then, week forty came and went. Now at turtle speed, I was entering week forty-one and I was getting nervous. My plan was always to avoid medicine or medical intervention, but because my little one loved being in utero as much as I did, my wants were becoming further and further from reality.

My midwives had decided that on the following Monday, I was going to be induced. My mom flew in from Minnesota to stay with us so she could be there with me a few days before the induction and then spend some days with her newest grandchild.

We had so much fun during those first few days. We walked around the mall (with a lot of pausing), ate lots of salty and spicy food (did I mention mango avocado rolls?), I drank over 8 ounces of castor oil every day, took herbs, and just enjoyed our final moments together as a family of two.

On Sunday after we got back from shopping, we were hanging out watching TV, where I was sitting on my oversized ball, trying to encourage the baby and my uterus to work in tandem so I wouldn't have to be induced the next night.

My mom suggested that I try some lunges and sure enough, one deep lunge later, a POP went off and a gush came running down my leg. I shrieked, wondering if my water had just broken, as I hobbled over to the bathroom to examine. Sure enough, it did.

*Oh, thank God! Thank you, Jesus and Halleluiah! *

On speaker phone, we called my midwife who proceeded to tell us in her calm and reassuring voice that my early labor was now beginning, and it was best if I tried to get some rest.

I sarcastically chuckled, "There's no way I can sleep. These contractions are already very strong and seven minutes apart."

The midwife suggested I take Benadryl to knock me out, but all it did was invoke the beast because I threw it up twenty seconds later and had a new wave of angry contractions come with a vengeance.

Very quickly, my contractions boosted from being seven minutes to five minutes apart. I was squirming on our bed, holding the bed frame as tightly as I could, moaning and groaning because of the sheer force of the contractions.

An hour had passed and my contractions escalated quickly to four minutes apart. On speaker again, we rang my midwife, Roxie, who calmly assured us, "She couldn't possibly be that far along already. I'll slowly start getting ready to head to the center but know, it'll take me an hour."

Worried that this train might be moving faster than my midwife, I continued this pattern for another four hours until finally, I got to a major turning point. I could no longer walk without taking one step and having a deep contraction.

Now around 2:30 am, my mom had to call the midwife this time to say, "Ready or not, we're heading to the birthing center. We will be there in thirty minutes."

I don't remember much about the car ride but I know it definitely didn't take us thirty minutes to get there. As Juan parked, I had one of my strongest contractions yet, which forced my body to push.

As soon as Juan ran over to my side of the car to open the door, I had another full-force contraction. This baby was on its way!

Juan picked me up and carried me through the door as Roxie met us at the two-door entrance. Quickly, the midwife and Juan walked me to the bed to see how dilated I was and sure enough, I was ready to birth a baby.

Shooing my mom out of the room and waiting for the tub to fill up, my contractions were now two minutes apart. I hopped into the tub to start actively pushing the baby, but unfortunately, the calming warm water only slowed down my progress.

Five full hours of pushing and getting turtle-like results, the moment had finally come. The photographer (boujee, I know, but it came with the room) showed me the baby's head, proving that our little one couldn't decide if it wanted to be in or out.

Apparently, we had been there for so many hours that it was time for the nurses to switch out.

This grey fox of a woman, who was clearly very experienced and wise, came in, saw what the situation was, and had me hold my legs back as far as they would go. Meanwhile, she jabbed her hand down into my stomach so forcefully, that that alone motivated me to push and get this baby out just so she would stop doing that.

One contraction and three pushes later, the baby came out and was laid onto my chest. After eleven hours of active labor, five hours of straight pushing, and no medicine during any of it, I felt on top of the world (wiped out but elated)!

I exclaimed, "What is it?" to which the nurse shrugged nonchalantly. Juan dove right into the baby's genitals and we discovered.... we had a baby boy!

Little Santiago Barreto came twelve days past his due day, one day before daddy's birthday, and on God's perfect timing!

* *

With Alba, I told them relatively early that I was pregnant because I had full faith that our baby was going full-term. I worked all the way up until a few weeks before my due date, as the constant standing and walking all those blocks to work started taking a toll.

The initial plan was to be a stay-at-home mom with Santi for four months then return to work, but God had other plans.

As I was adjusting to being a new mommy, with the around the clock pumping and breastfeeding, all day bonding and lack of sleep, I couldn't imagine leaving my little man so soon. The bond we had created was unfathomable. I kept telling Juan how I wanted to push my time going back to work from five months to six. Then six turned to seven.

I thought that in the meantime, I'd just keep writing and focusing on my book, but the reality was, being pregnant took a lot of energy out of me, which only slowed down the process. Then, once I had a newborn, there was no extra space for anything, especially writing. Simply taking a shower was a real metric of success for the day.

But as Santi was getting to be three months, I thought things were becoming easier; He was sleeping throughout the night, I was finding consistent windows to shower, taking daily walks around Hoboken, and joining weekly mommy/baby groups.

With my new post-partum swagger, I felt that I was getting the hang of my new title. I was so looking forward to the next year: watching my baby grow exponentially, taking a grand vacation abroad to Asia as a family of three, becoming a published author, and jumping from state to state doing publicity tours.

I just knew 2020 was going to be a great year, filled with adventure, fresh air, and trusting where God wanted to take me. No surprises were going to take me down!

New adventure

* Coronavirus? Wait, what's that? *

To be continued....

Acknowledgements

Without God in my life, this book never would have been written. Without God, the testimonies that I've shared would have been credited to coincidences. I thank Him for everything that has happened and will happen in my life. I thank Him for answering my wild prayers and going above and beyond. I thank God for caring about my interests, hopes, and desires. And most importantly, I thank God every day for using me to be a part of His kingdom.

I am so grateful to my amazing husband, Juan, who has been alongside of me through my writing, career transitions, doubts, and God-centered dreams. I cannot thank him enough for his constant support and fearless approach to life, along with kicking me in the butt when I need it. I am forever grateful to you, mi amor, and our incredible partnership that we have built.

To my beautiful baby boy, I pray that you will grow up seeing parents who not only love you incredibly, but who show you a God whose love is so much grander than we could ever express. I pray that you would know that everything I do; I do for you. I love you with my entire heart and soul, now and forever. You, my angel, are God's precious gift and mommy's answered prayer.

I want to thank my family for their encouragement through all these wild and crazy dreams that started when I was just a pre-teen. Your constant questioning and check-ins were much appreciated and needed.

To my friends, you hold a special place in my heart, and I can never thank you enough for your kind words and accountability, especially when I needed them most. Without you all, I wouldn't be where I am today. You mean the world to me.

I don't think I could have done any of this without the incredible Rachel C. Swanson, my mentor and guide through this writing process; I am forever indebted to you. Thank you to David Miles, who is blessed with beautiful creativity and used his gifts to craft my cover art. Thank you to my editor, Jennie Scott, who did an incredible job helping me through the process, and always with a beautiful spirit.

And I want to thank you, the reader, from the bottom of my heart. Whatever you got out of this book, know that I wrote it for you. I wrote it so that you could see how much God loves and craves you. I wrote this so you could be encouraged to know that He is active in your life. I want nothing more for you than to have a relationship with Him. I pray that you will take leaps and bounds for Him when He has consistently done the same for us. So again, to all, thank you from the bottom of my heart.

Made in the USA
Middletown, DE
04 March 2021